AF552134

# The Bhagavad Gita for Children

An Imprint of Om Books International

Om SHAKTI An Imprint of Om Books International

Reprinted in 2026

**Corporate & Editorial Office**
A-12, Sector 64, Noida 201 301
Uttar Pradesh, India
Phone: +91 120 477 4100
Email: editorial@ombooks.com
Website: www.ombooksinternational.com

**Sales Office**
107, Ansari Road, Darya Ganj
New Delhi 110 002, India
Phone: +91 11 4000 9000
Email: sales@ombooks.com



ISBN: 978-93-8160-750-3

Printed in India

10 9 8 7 6 5 4 3 2

# Contents

# Introduction to the Bhagavad Gita

The Srimad Bhagavad Gita is the dialogue between Lord Krishna and Arjuna, which has been narrated in the Bheeshma Parva of the Mahabharata. The Bhagavad Gita is composed of eighteen discourses in Sanskrit. Lord Krishna has revealed the most beautiful, intense and soul-searching spiritual truths through the Bhagavad Gita. As the sacred book of the Hindus, the Gita has passed on its wisdom and teachings from generation to generation since time immemorial. The value of the Gita does not lie in the language it is written in, but in the brilliance of its content. No wonder that the Bhagavad Gita is one of the finest world-scriptures today, guiding the lives of people

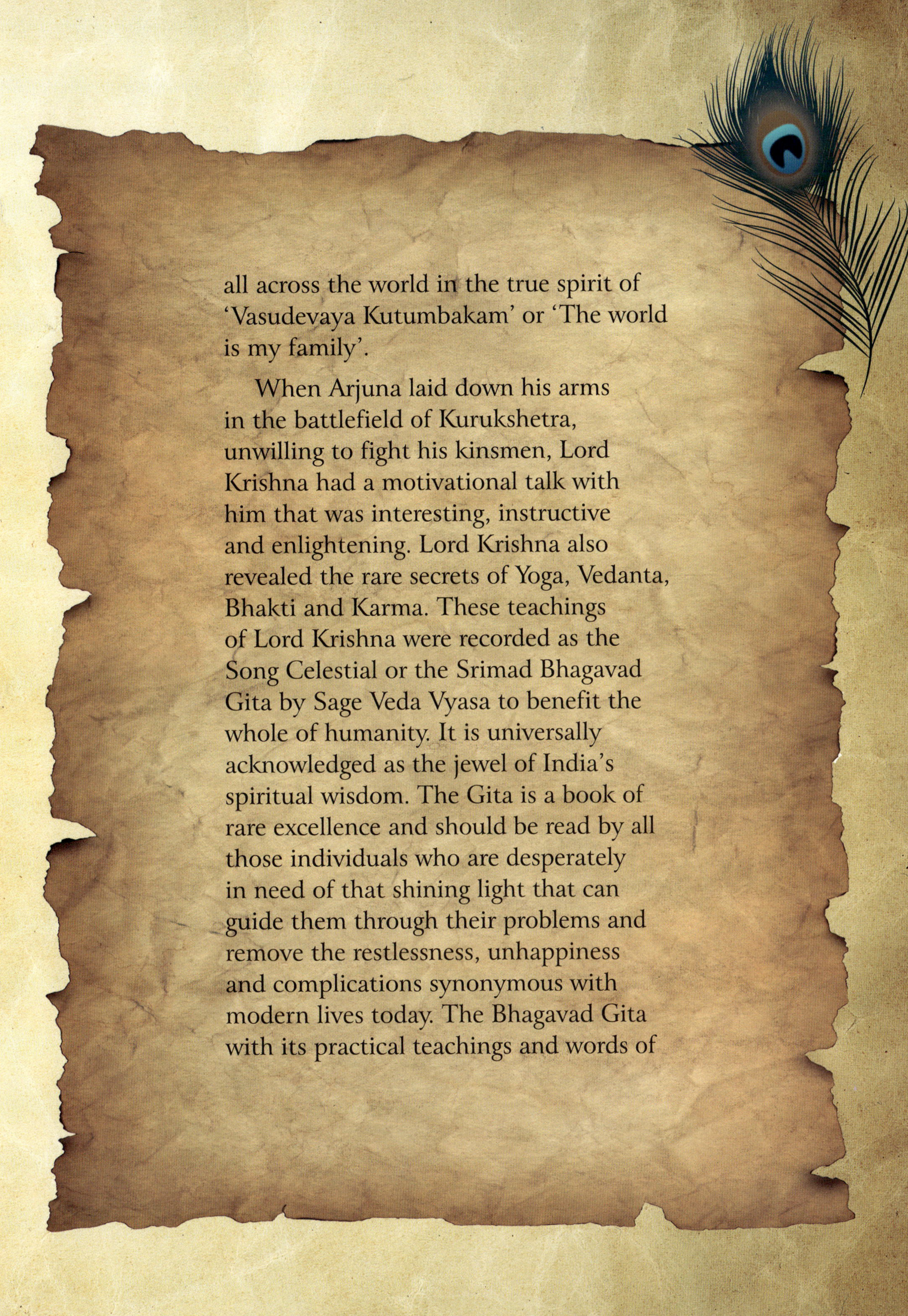

all across the world in the true spirit of 'Vasudevaya Kutumbakam' or 'The world is my family'.

When Arjuna laid down his arms in the battlefield of Kurukshetra, unwilling to fight his kinsmen, Lord Krishna had a motivational talk with him that was interesting, instructive and enlightening. Lord Krishna also revealed the rare secrets of Yoga, Vedanta, Bhakti and Karma. These teachings of Lord Krishna were recorded as the Song Celestial or the Srimad Bhagavad Gita by Sage Veda Vyasa to benefit the whole of humanity. It is universally acknowledged as the jewel of India's spiritual wisdom. The Gita is a book of rare excellence and should be read by all those individuals who are desperately in need of that shining light that can guide them through their problems and remove the restlessness, unhappiness and complications synonymous with modern lives today. The Bhagavad Gita with its practical teachings and words of

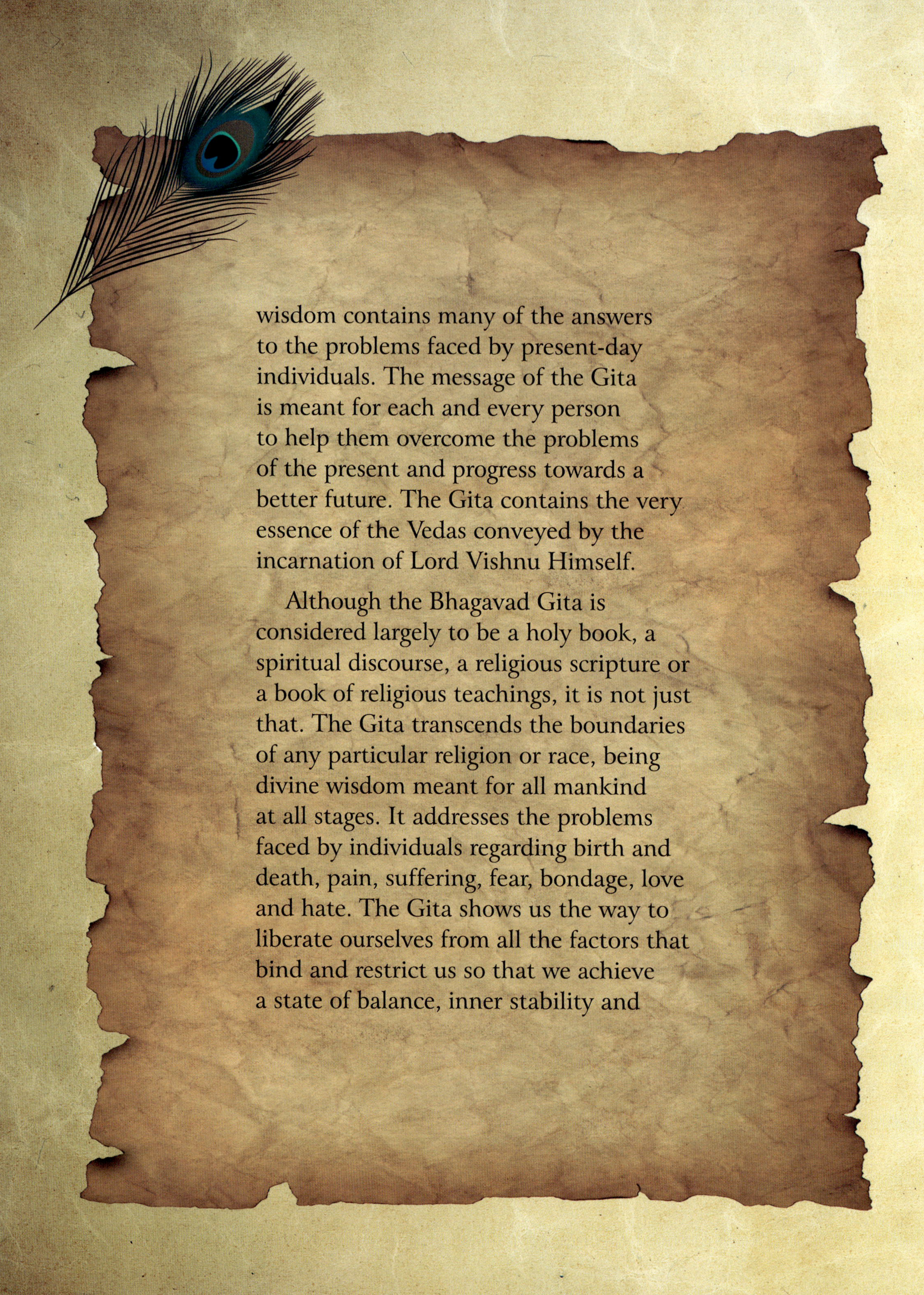

wisdom contains many of the answers to the problems faced by present-day individuals. The message of the Gita is meant for each and every person to help them overcome the problems of the present and progress towards a better future. The Gita contains the very essence of the Vedas conveyed by the incarnation of Lord Vishnu Himself.

Although the Bhagavad Gita is considered largely to be a holy book, a spiritual discourse, a religious scripture or a book of religious teachings, it is not just that. The Gita transcends the boundaries of any particular religion or race, being divine wisdom meant for all mankind at all stages. It addresses the problems faced by individuals regarding birth and death, pain, suffering, fear, bondage, love and hate. The Gita shows us the way to liberate ourselves from all the factors that bind and restrict us so that we achieve a state of balance, inner stability and

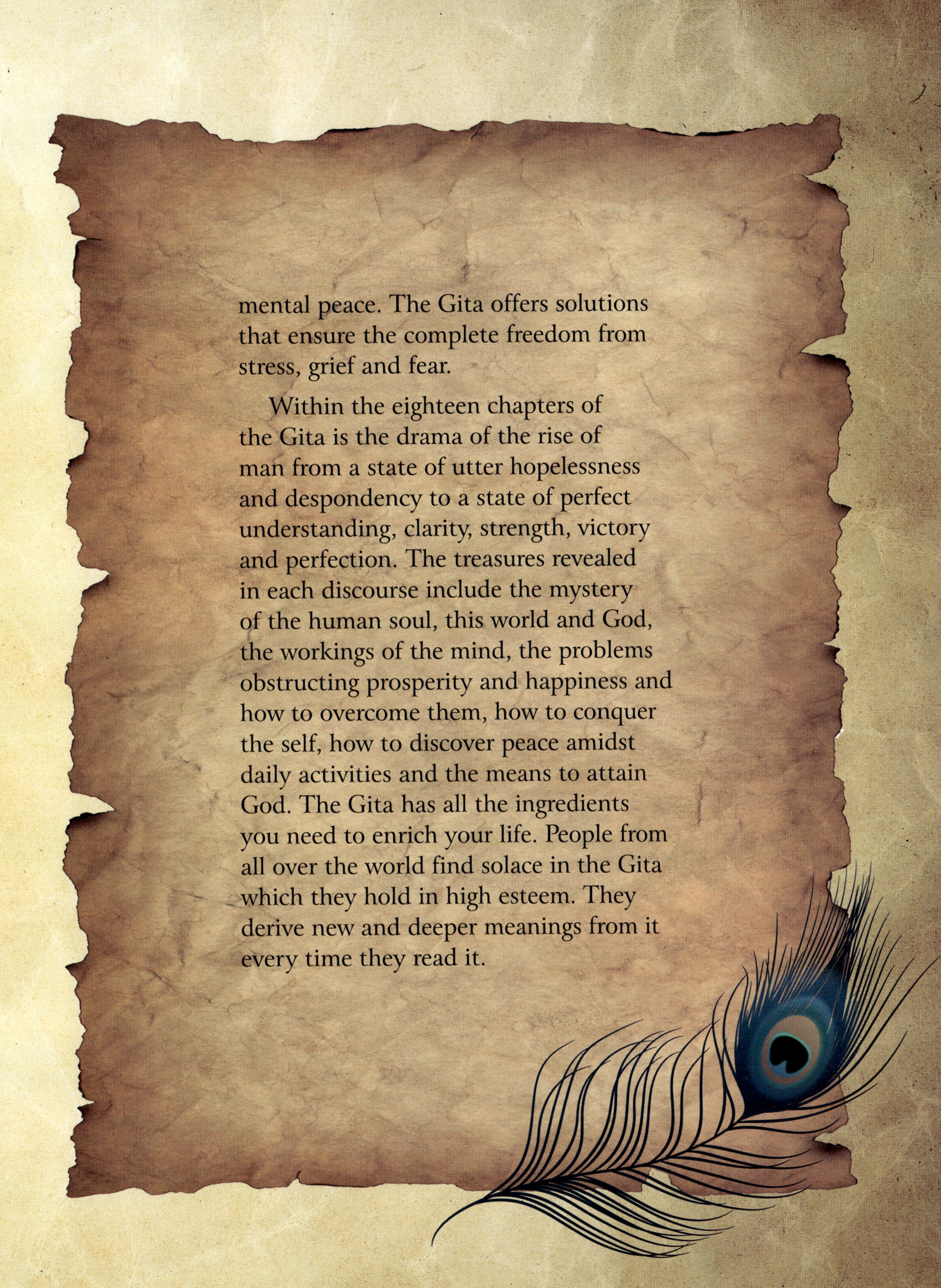

mental peace. The Gita offers solutions that ensure the complete freedom from stress, grief and fear.

Within the eighteen chapters of the Gita is the drama of the rise of man from a state of utter hopelessness and despondency to a state of perfect understanding, clarity, strength, victory and perfection. The treasures revealed in each discourse include the mystery of the human soul, this world and God, the workings of the mind, the problems obstructing prosperity and happiness and how to overcome them, how to conquer the self, how to discover peace amidst daily activities and the means to attain God. The Gita has all the ingredients you need to enrich your life. People from all over the world find solace in the Gita which they hold in high esteem. They derive new and deeper meanings from it every time they read it.

# Prayers

## Prayer to Veda Vyasa

*Namostu te vyaasa visaalabuddhe phullaaravindaa yatapatranetra,*
*Yena twayaa bhaaratatailapoornah prajwaalito jnaanamayah pradeepah.*

Salutations to thee, O Vyasa, of great intellect and with eyes that are large as the petals of a lotus in full bloom, by the grace of whom the lamp of divine knowledge, filled with the oil of the Mahabharata, has been lighted!

## Prayer to the Guru

*Gururbrahmaa gururvishnurgururdevo maheshwarah; Guruh saakshaat param brahma tasmai shree gurave namah.*

The Guru is the Creator of the Three Worlds, Lord Brahma. The Guru is the Preserver Lord Vishnu. The Guru is the Destroyer Maheshvara or Lord Shiva. The Guru is the Supreme Absolute and we pray to that Guru.

*Dhyaanamoolam gurormoortih poojaamoolam guroh padam;*
*Mantramoolam gurorvaakyam mokshamoolam guroh kripaa.*

The form of the Guru is the very root of meditation. The Guru's feet form the root of worship, the word of the Guru is the root of Mantra and the root of Moksha or salvation is the Guru's grace.

## Prayer to Lord Krishna

*Krishnaaya vaasudevaaya devakeenandanaaya cha;*
*Nandagopakumaaraaya govindaaya namo namah.*

I bow again and again to Lord Krishna, son of Vasudeva and Devaki, the darling of Nandagopa and the protector of cows.

# A Brief History of the Mahabharata

## 1

## Veda Vyasa Meets Lord Ganesha

The Mahabharata is Veda Vyasa's legendary epic on the Kuru dynasty. When the great Sage Veda Vyasa decided to compose this epic poem, he requested the god of wisdom, Lord Ganesha to be the scribe of his epic as he recited it. Lord Ganesha agreed on one condition.

"Maharishi, if there is any pause in your reciting of the shlokas and my pen stops as a result, I shall abandon the task and leave immediately," Lord Ganesha stated. Vyasa had no option but to agree as it was not possible for him to write such a lengthy epic on his own.

"I agree on one condition, O Lord Ganesha," Vyasa replied. "Whatever I recite, you shall not write it down without comprehending its depth and meaning."

Lord Ganesha agreed and the recitation and writing of the Mahabharata began. Veda Vyasa began the longest dictation that has ever been made. Veda Vyasa would use a difficult shloka when he needed to take a break. As Lord Ganesha would scratch his head to figure out the words, Veda Vyasa would take a deep breath of fresh air and quickly gulp down some water. This is how the great epic, the Mahabharata was composed and penned down.

# 2

## Dushyant and Shakuntala

Veda Vyasa set the tone of the Mahabharata with the love story of the beautiful Shakuntala and the powerful King Dushyant. One day, King Dushyant was on a hunting trip in the forest when he met the beautiful Shakuntala near her hermitage of Sage Kanva. The two of them fell in love and got married by exchanging garlands.

"I have to return to my palace now," Dushyant said to Shakuntala after a few days. "But I shall send an envoy to escort you there as my queen."

As a parting gift, Dushyant handed over his royal ring to Shakuntala.

"Here," Dushyant said to Shakuntala. "Always wear this ring. This royal souvenir will serve as the evidence that you are my wife."

One day, the Sage Durvasa arrived at Shakuntala's hermitage. Durvasa was notorious for his fiery temper and cursing people for minor faults. Shakuntala was so lost in her thoughts about Dushyant that she failed to notice the divine sage when he called out to her, thus incurring Durvasa's wrath.

"How dare you ignore me?" Durvasa thundered in rage. "I hereby curse you that the very person about whom you are thinking right now, will fail to recognise you!"

Shakuntala's friends quickly came to her rescue and told Durvasa the reason of her distraction. Durvasa relented and added a condition to his curse.

"He will be able to recall you when you produce a suitable souvenir," Durvasa declared.

# 3

## The Discovery of the Lost Ring

Shakuntala was worried when the days turned to weeks and yet, no one arrived from Dushyant's palace to fetch her.

*Let me go to Hastinapura and meet King Dushyant to remind him about our matrimonial vows,* Shakuntala decided. There was another reason for Shakuntala's anxiety. She was pregnant with Dushyant's child and wanted Dushyant to accept them both.

But as Shakuntala travelled to Hastinapura, she accidentally dropped Dushyant's ring in the river where it was swallowed by a fish.

"Oh, no!" Shakuntala exclaimed.

Because of Durvasa's curse, Dushyant failed to recognise Shakuntala, who left his palace in tears. Soon, Shakuntala gave birth to Dushyant's son who grew up in the ashram.

Years later, an excited fisherman arrived at Dushyant's court to display before the king a ring he had discovered in the stomach of his catch. As Dushyant examined the ring, the memories came rushing back!

It was the same ring that he had given Shakuntala which she had lost in the river.

"Oh Shakuntala!" Dushyant exclaimed, and rushed to Sage Kanva's ashram.

# 4

## Bharata and Shantanu

As he neared the ashram, Dushyant was greeted by a strange sight. He saw a young boy staring inside the mouth of a ferocious lion and counting its teeth.

*Who is this brave child?* A stunned Dushyant wondered.

"Who are you, my son?" Dushyant asked the boy.

"My name is Bharata," the boy replied.

"Who are your parents?" Dushyant asked.

"I am the son of Shakuntala," the boy stated, and Dushyant trembled with excitement.

*Could this be my son?* He thought.

"Can you take me to your mother?" Dushyant requested Bharata who led him to Shakuntala. Dushyant was finally reunited with his wife and son who accompanied him to Hastinapura.

In due course, Bharata inherited the throne from Dushyant and expanded his kingdom right from the Himalayas to the Oceans. The land was renamed Bharatavarsha after the mighty king Bharata.

The circumstances that led to the Mahabharata begin with the tale of King Shantanu, a descendant of King Bharata. One day, Shantanu spotted the Goddess Ganga on the banks of the holy river Ganga. Shantanu was dazzled by her beauty and fell in love at first sight.

"Will you marry me?" he asked Goddess Ganga. She accepted his proposal on one condition.

"O King, you must promise that you will never ask me to explain my actions after we are married," the goddess declared. Shantanu accepted readily.

# 5

## Shantanu and Ganga

Shantanu and Goddess Ganga got married. Soon, Goddess Ganga gave birth to a child. Shantanu was horrified when she cast away the infant into the River Ganga. But he was bound by his promise not to question her. Ganga gave birth to many children but cast them all into the holy river and returned to Shantanu with a smiling face, who remained a mute spectator. But Shantanu could not control himself when Ganga was about to fling their eighth child into the river.

"Stop!" he exclaimed. "What are you doing?"

When he questioned his wife about her weird actions, Ganga revealed that she had married Shantanu to give birth to eight demi-gods who had been cursed to be born as humans.

"By throwing them into the river, I was relieving them of the curse," Ganga explained. Ganga left for heaven with the eighth child, promising to return him at the right time. When she did, Shantanu named his son Devavrata, who later came to be known as Bheeshma.

Years later, the wifeless Shantanu fell in love with Satyavati, the daughter of the chief of fishermen. Shantanu approached Satyavati's father for her hand in marriage. The fisherman gave his consent on one condition—the son born to Satyavati would inherit Shantanu's throne.

# 6

## Bheeshma's Vow

As Shantanu's natural successor to the throne was his eldest son Devavrata, there was no way that he could agree to the fisherman's proposal. He returned to the palace a broken-hearted man because of his failure to marry Satyavati. Devavrata noticed that his father was sad and distracted, and discovered the reason behind Shantanu's anguish. He went and met Satyavati's father to assure him that Satyavati's son would ascend the throne.

"Give your daughter's hand in marriage to my father. I promise you that I shall never ascend the throne of Hastinapur!" Devavrata vowed."The son of Satyavati will inherit the throne from my father."

"You might not, but your children might want to become kings after you," the cunning fisherman replied.

"I shall never marry till I die," Devavrata vowed. At this great vow of brahmacharya or celibacy, that involved total sacrifice, the devas showered flowers on Devavrata from the Heavens above.

Because of this great vow, he came to be known as Bheeshma. (The one who takes a difficult vow and fulfils it.)

Shantanu and Satyavati were finally married and had two sons named Chitrangad and Vichitravirya. Chitrangad ascended the throne after Shantanu but died on the battlefield. As he was childless, he was succeeded by Vichitravirya who ruled Hastinapur under the able guidance of his elder step-brother, the mighty Bheeshma.

# 7

## The Kuru Dynasty

Vichitravirya died leaving behind his two wives Ambika and Ambalika without an heir to the throne.

"Marry Ambika and Ambalika and become the king of Hastinapur," Satyavati requested Bheeshma.

"I am afraid I cannot do that as I have taken the vow of celibacy and promised your father that I shall never ascend the throne of Hastinapur," Bheeshma replied.

To save the kingdom, the Queen Mother Satyavati summoned her eldest son Vyasa, whom she had borne after a boon from the gods. She ordered Vyasa to bless Ambika and Ambalika with children. When Vyasa approached Ambika, she closed her eyes in fright after seeing the sage's frightening appearance. As a result, the son born to her was blind and was named Dhritarashtra. When Ambalika arrived before Vyasa, she turned pale on seeing his dreadful appearance. The son born to Ambalika was pale and unhealthy as a result and was named Pandu. Satyavati requested Vyasa for another child who was more suitable to rule the kingdom. But Ambika and Ambalika were too scared to face Vyasa again, and sent their maid to him instead, in the cover of darkness. The son born to this maid was both healthy and intelligent. He was named Vidura and served as the prime minister of both Dhritarashtra and Pandu.

Dhritarashtra was married to Gandhari who blindfolded herself permanently since the day of her wedding in solidarity with her blind husband. Thanks to a boon that the pious Gandhari had received from Lord Shiva, she and Dhritarashtra had a hundred sons known as the Kauravas. The five sons of Pandu and his queens Kunti and Madri were called the Pandavas.

# 8

## The Birth of the Pandavas

When Dhritarashtra was about to be crowned as the king of Hastinapur, the wise Vidura intervened.

"A blind man cannot be the ruler of a kingdom," Vidura, who was well-versed in court practices and policies, explained the logic behind his statement. Therefore, it was decided that Dhritarashtra's younger brother Pandu would ascend the throne. So, Pandu was crowned the king of Hastinapur.

One day, as he was hunting in the forest, Pandu accidentally shot a sage who was with his wife.

"You shall die if you touch your wives again," the sage cursed Pandu before his death. A dejected Pandu gave up the throne to Dhritarashtra and retired to the forest with his wives to meditate.

Pandu's first wife Kunti had received a boon from the Sage Durvasa that allowed her to bear children from any god she chose to. She shared this secret with Pandu who encouraged her and Madri to invoke this boon so that his royal lineage could continue. Madri invoked the Ashwini twins and bore the twins named Nakula and Sahadeva.

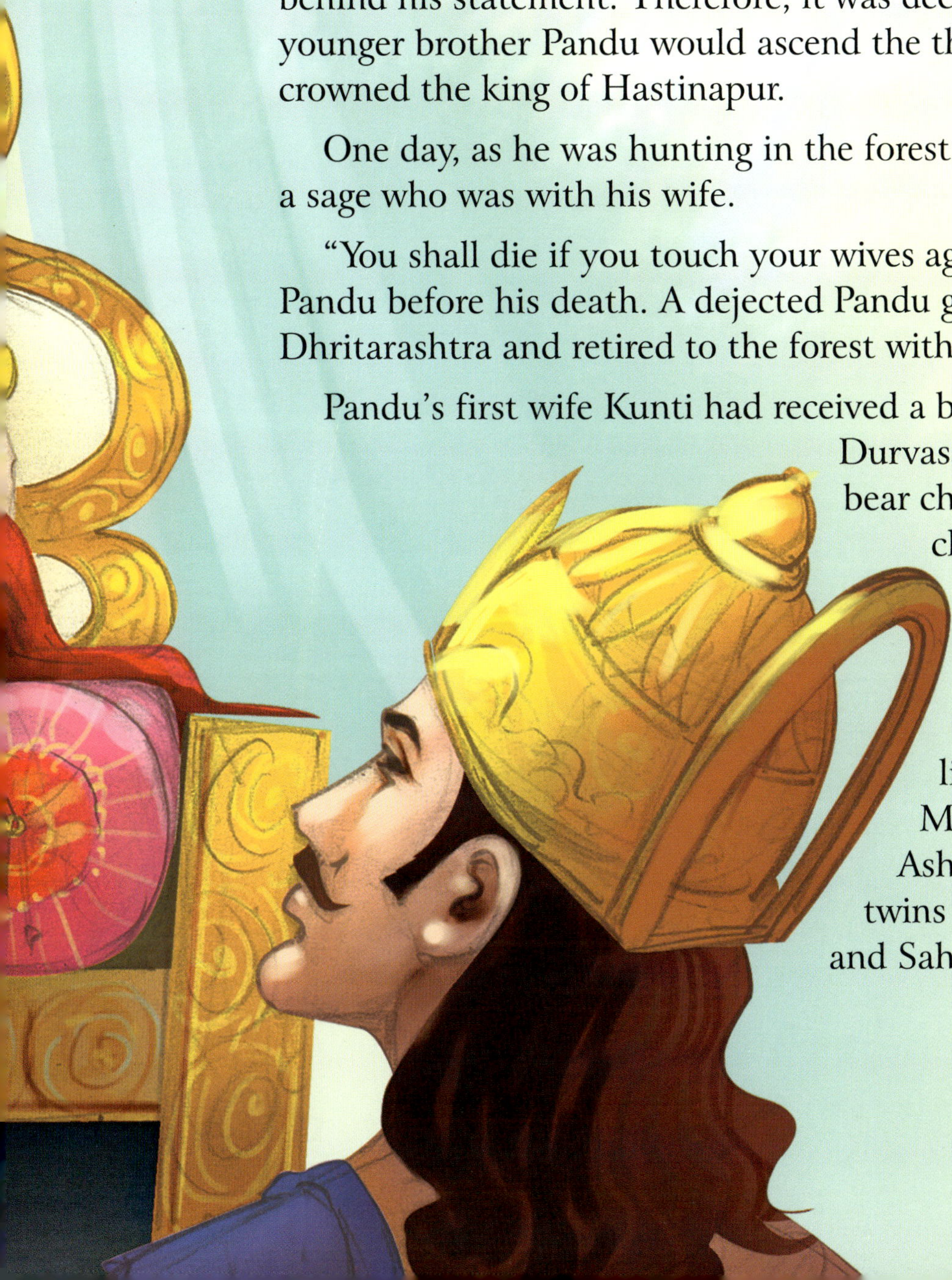

# 9

## The Treachery of the Kauravas

Kunti bore three sons. Her eldest son Yudhishthira was born by the grace of Dharma, the god of justice. Bheema's father was Vayu, the god of wind and Arjuna was born thanks to Lord Indra.

Pandu and his family lived happily in the forest before an untoward incident led to his death. The sage's curse came true when Pandu got intimate with his queen Madri in a moment of weakness and died. Madri considered herself responsible for her husband's death and decided to commit Sati on her dead husband's funeral pyre, thus ending her own life as well.

Kunti and the Pandavas returned to Hastinapur after Pandu and Madri died. Yudhishthira was anointed the Crown Prince of Hastinapur being Pandu's eldest son and the rightful heir to the throne according to the laws of the land. But Dhritarashtra's eldest son Duryodhana was dead against the idea of Yudhishthira becoming the king of Hastinapur.

"The throne belongs to me," Duryodhana exclaimed, and hatched an evil plot with his uncle Shakuni to kill the Pandavas. Duryodhana built a palace that was inflammable and would burn down quickly as soon as it was torched. Then, he invited Kunti and the Pandavas to stay in it as his guests. But Kunti and the Pandavas escaped, thanks to Vidura, who had got to know about Duryodhana's evil plan and informed the Pandavas of the same. As Duryodhana's men burnt the palace to ashes, Kunti and the Pandavas escaped to the forest through a secret exit. People in Hastinapur mourned the deaths of Kunti and the Pandavas as everybody thought they had succumbed to the fire.

The Pandavas lived in the forest with their mother, encountering many hardships and dangers. Sage Vyasa met them in the forest and advised them to be disguised as brahmins. The Pandavas were residing in a place named Ekachakrapura when they heard about the swayamvara of Draupadi, the beautiful daughter of King Drupada of Panchala.

# 10

## Draupadi's Swayamvara

The Pandavas attended Draupadi's swayamvara disguised as brahmins, in which Arjuna won the archery contest to win Draupadi's hand. This happened after all the mighty Kshatriyas, including the Kauravas, had failed to hit the difficult target. Draupadi had refused to let Karna participate in the contest mocking at him for being the son of a charioteer. The Kauravas and other Kshatriya warriors were angry that a brahmin had defeated them. They attacked King Drupada in anger but were defeated by the Pandavas.

The Pandavas returned with Draupadi to their hut.

"Mother, look what we've got for you," they shouted from outside. Kunti commanded her sons from inside to share equally among themselves whatever they had brought. The Pandavas were forced to marry Draupadi following their mother's command. Following this marriage, the Pandavas found a strong ally in Draupadi's father, Drupada and his son Dhrishtadyumna.

Soon, news reached Hastinapur that Kunti and the Pandavas were alive and they were brought back to the palace. As per the advice of the Kuru elders like Bheeshma, Vidura, Drona and Kripacharya, Dhritarashtra decided to pacify both Duryodhana and the Pandavas. The might of the Pandavas also scared Dhritarashtra. It was decided that the kingdom would be divided into two equal halves.

"Duryodhana will rule from his capital at Hastinapur and Yudhishthira will have his capital at Khandavaprastha," Dhritarashtra declared. The Pandavas accepted this proposal.

# 11

## The Game of Dice

Everyone was pleased when Kunti and the Pandavas returned to Hastinapur except Duryodhana and the Kauravas. The Pandavas set up their capital a little distance away from Hastinapur and named it Indraprastha. Arjuna had saved the asura named Maya from being burnt alive by Lord Agni in the Khandava forest. To repay this debt, Maya, who was the architect of the asuras, built a splendid palace for the Pandavas which was one of a kind. After the palace was completed, everyone in Hastinapur was invited there, including the Kauravas.

Duryodhana was awestruck but jealous to see this beautiful palace of illusions and splendour. The floor was so glossy in one area that Duryodhana thought it was a pool of water, and refused to walk over it. Later, Duryodhana mistook another area for a glossy floor which was actually a pool of water. He fell straight into it with a splash as he walked over it.

"Ha, ha!" Draupadi laughed at Duryodhana's plight. "He is blind just like his father!" she exclaimed.

*I shall take my revenge against this humiliation!* Duryodhana vowed angrily. Duryodhana's maternal uncle, the wicked Shakuni had formed another plan to get rid of the Pandavas so that Duryodhana could become the king of the entire land.

"Go and invite Yudhishthira for a game of dice," Shakuni advised Duryodhana, aware of Yudhishthira's addiction to gambling. "We shall defeat them in the game of dice and send them to live in exile in the forest!"

In the game of dice, Yudhishthira lost his entire wealth and kingdom to Duryodhana. Shakuni, who played on Duryodhana's behalf, used his treachery with the dice to win. Yudhishthira staked all his brothers and Draupadi in the dice game, who became Duryodhana's slaves. Only a miracle by Lord Krishna saved Draupadi from utter humiliation by Dushasana who acted upon Duryodhana's orders.

# 12

## The Pandavas in Exile

When Bheema threatened to kill the Kauravas and destroy their entire race for humiliating Draupadi, Dhritarashtra was scared. He returned everything that Yudhishthira had lost in the dice game and asked him to return to his kingdom Indraprastha. But after the Pandavas left, Duryodhana argued with his father and convinced him that the Pandavas should be invited for another game of dice.

"If they win, the Pandavas get back their kingdom and if they lose, they shall be banished for twelve years to live in exile in the forest," Duryodhana declared. Dhritarashtra, who loved his wicked son unconditionally, agreed reluctantly, and the Pandavas were summoned for yet another game of dice. Shakuni defeated Yudhishthira yet again. According to the condition, the Pandavas would have to live the next thirteen years of their lives in exile and the final year of their exile would be spent in hiding. If they were found and recognised during this last year, they would have to spend another twelve years in exile.

For the next twelve years, the Pandavas travelled throughout the length and breadth of the kingdom. In the final year of their exile, they sought refuge in the kingdom of Virata in disguise and served the king. After the period of exile, Duryodhana refused to return the kingdom to the Pandavas. The elders of the court like Vidura and Bheeshma pleaded with Dhritarashtra to convince Duryodhana to avoid war. But the blind king had lost all control over his son.

"If the Pandavas want the kingdom, they have to fight for it," Duryodhana declared. Lord Krishna was sent as Yudhishthira's envoy to negotiate with the Kauravas to avoid war. But he failed as Duryodhana refused to come to a settlement with the Pandavas, even refusing to give them five villages as requested. The only word on Duryodhana's lips was WAR!!!

# 13

## The Battle of Kurukshetra

It was clear that war was inevitable now between the Pandavas and the Kauravas as both the sides failed to come to an agreement. The elders of Hastinapur including Dhritarashtra, Bheeshma, Vidura and Dronacharya—all tried to make Duryodhana understand the repercussions of war. But all of them failed as Duryodhana was adamant about the war with the Pandavas.

War was finally declared and the fields of Kurukshetra were chosen as the venue for the Great War of the Mahabharata. Both sides started recruiting the kings of the land to join their side in this war. Vidura decided to remain neutral and Lord Krishna declared that he would not play an active role in this war but would serve as Arjuna's charioteer.

As the two armies faced each other in battle, Arjuna faced a moral dilemma of fighting with his relatives and confessed the same to Lord Krishna. Lord Krishna gave him a sermon to dispel his doubts and calm his agitated mind. This discourse is known as the Bhagavad Gita, which has been accepted worldwide as the Song of God.

The Bhagavad Gita is regarded as one of the supreme treasures of world literature. It is a message of devotion to duty without any attachments, desires or expectation of rewards. The Bhagavad Gita teaches that all men and women should do the right regardless of whether they are rich or poor, learned or ignorant. It is the source of light amidst the darkness and the problems of life. The Bhagavad Gita is the spiritual essence of the Mahabharata.

The Bhagavad Gita

Chapter One

# Arjuna Vishad Yoga

## (The Despondency of Arjuna)

### Summary of the First Discourse

The great war of the Mahabharata took place on the battlefield of Kurukshetra between the Pandavas and the Kauravas. The famous and mighty warriors from both sides faced each other on the battlefield mounted on their resplendent chariots and elephants. Arjuna's magnificent chariot, yoked with sturdy white horses arrived on the battlefield. It was none other than Lord Krishna who was acting as Arjuna's charioteer, seated at the helm of this chariot with the great Hanuman sitting on the flag, protecting the vehicle. In the midst of the din were hundreds of conches blown by warriors from both sides to herald the beginning of this Great War.

"O Krishna, can you please take my chariot closer to the Kaurava army so that I may survey my opponents before the battle begins?" Arjuna requested Lord Krishna. Lord Krishna obliged, and placed the chariot right between the two armies. Arjuna was stunned and bewildered when he looked at his opponents. Instead of enemies, he saw brothers, elders, grandfathers, *gurus*, relatives and friends in the Kaurava army. A sudden confusion invaded Arjuna's mind and his self-assurance disappeared.

*Should I participate in this terrible war?* He thought. *Is it right on my part to kill my own relatives to gain the kingdom? Wouldn't it be better for me to avoid this sin of killing my own relatives and surrender everything to retire in peace?*

A feeling of great despondency crept into Arjuna's troubled mind as he lost all his enthusiasm to participate in the battle. His bow, the Gandeeva slipped away from his hands as he turned to Lord Krishna for advice and guidance.

Meanwhile, the father of the Kauravas, the blind king Dhritarashtra relied on the divine version of Sanjay, the son of Maharishi Vyasa, to narrate the happenings on the battlefield to him.

"O Sanjaya," Dhritarashtra enquired. "What did the armies of the sons of Pandu and my sons do after assembling on the battlefield of Kurukshetra?"

"Having seen the army of the Pandavas, King Duryodhana approached Guru Dronacharya and spoke these words," Sanjaya replied. "Behold the mighty army of the sons of Pandu, which has been ably organised by your pupil, Dhrishtdyumna, the son of King Drupada. Apart from Arjuna and Bheema, they have mighty warriors who match them like Yuyudhana, Virata and Drupada. They also have unrivalled warriors like Drishtaketu, Chekitana, the valiant king of Kasi, Kuntibhoja and Saibya. Abhimanyu, the son of Arjuna and the sons of the Pandavas are also great warriors. I fear that despite our army having so many heroes and led by Grandsire Bheeshma himself,

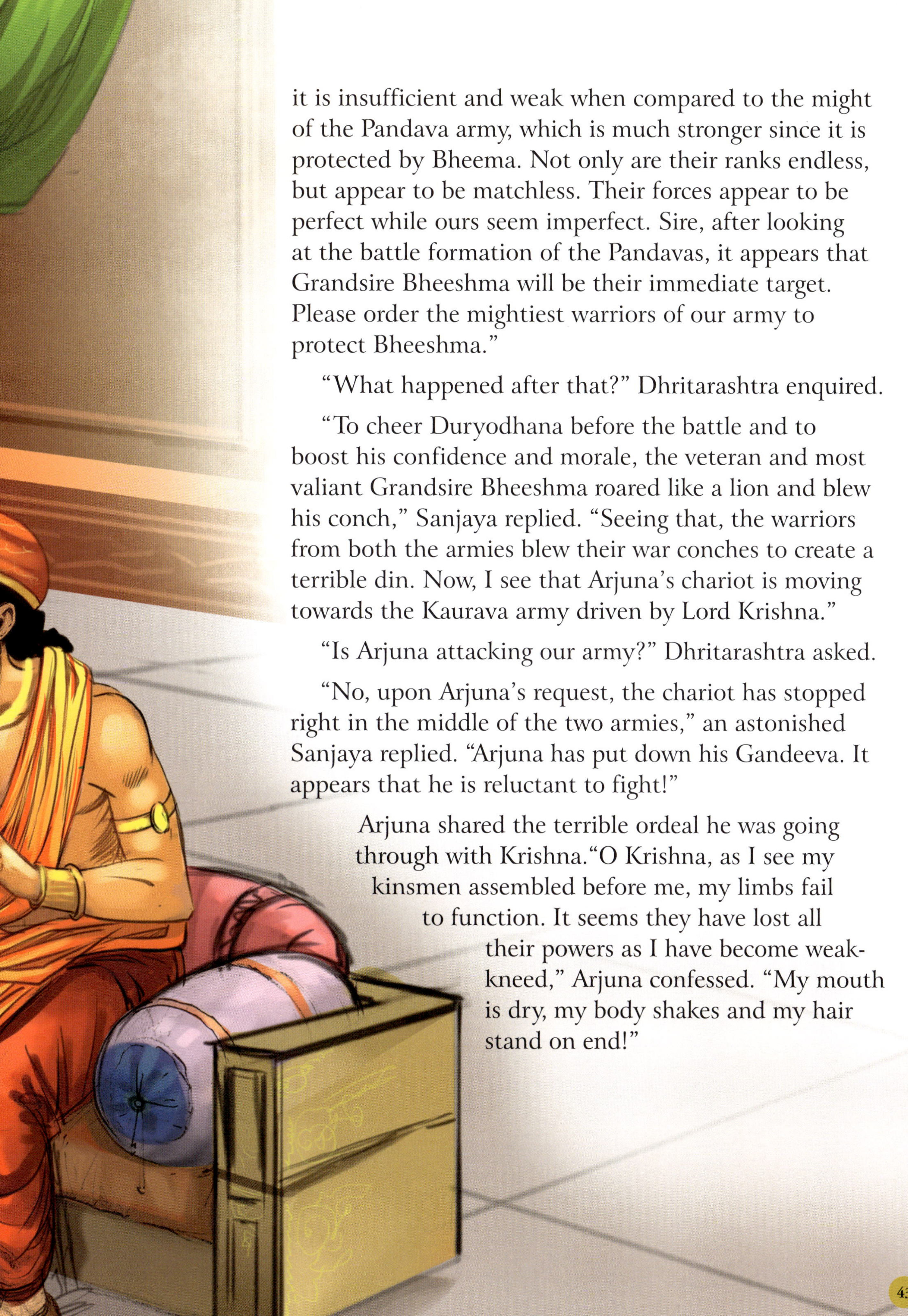

it is insufficient and weak when compared to the might of the Pandava army, which is much stronger since it is protected by Bheema. Not only are their ranks endless, but appear to be matchless. Their forces appear to be perfect while ours seem imperfect. Sire, after looking at the battle formation of the Pandavas, it appears that Grandsire Bheeshma will be their immediate target. Please order the mightiest warriors of our army to protect Bheeshma."

"What happened after that?" Dhritarashtra enquired.

"To cheer Duryodhana before the battle and to boost his confidence and morale, the veteran and most valiant Grandsire Bheeshma roared like a lion and blew his conch," Sanjaya replied. "Seeing that, the warriors from both the armies blew their war conches to create a terrible din. Now, I see that Arjuna's chariot is moving towards the Kaurava army driven by Lord Krishna."

"Is Arjuna attacking our army?" Dhritarashtra asked.

"No, upon Arjuna's request, the chariot has stopped right in the middle of the two armies," an astonished Sanjaya replied. "Arjuna has put down his Gandeeva. It appears that he is reluctant to fight!"

Arjuna shared the terrible ordeal he was going through with Krishna."O Krishna, as I see my kinsmen assembled before me, my limbs fail to function. It seems they have lost all their powers as I have become weak-kneed," Arjuna confessed. "My mouth is dry, my body shakes and my hair stand on end!"

*Arjuna said: Gaandeevam sramsate hastaat twak chaiva paridahyate; Na cha shaknomyavasthaatum bhramateeva cha me manah.*

***(The Gandeeva slips from my hand and there is a burning sensation all over my body. My mind reels and wanders and I am unable to stand properly on this chariot).***

"I do not see any benefit coming out of killing my own kin in battle," Arjuna confessed to Lord Krishna."Neither do I crave for victory in this battle and nor do I wish for kingdoms or pleasures at the cost of killing my own family members. We cannot derive any pleasure or benefit out of killing the Kauravas. We shall only incur sin! How can I forget the kindness of King Dhritarashtra, who raised us like his own children after our father Pandu's untimely death? How can I engage in battle with his sons today? The wisdom of the Kauravas has been eclipsed by their greed, and so they see no evil or sin in fighting and killing their own family members. But should we too follow their example instead of turning away from this sin? Once a race faces decline, the ancient morality associated with the race dies as well. When immorality sets in, the women of the race grow corrupt, thereby tainting the entire race which finds a permanent place in Hell.

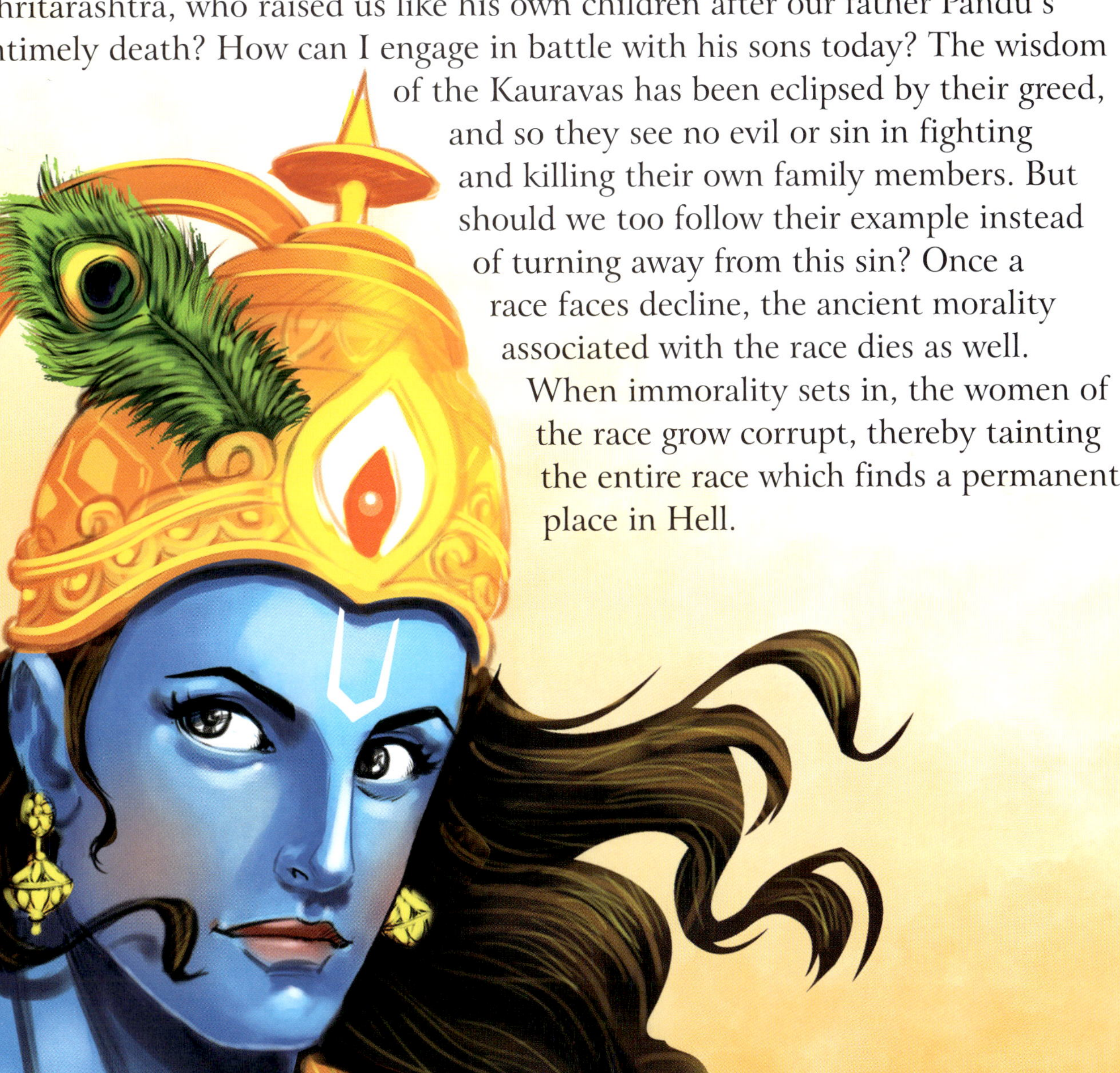

"If we do not distinguish between good and evil, there will be no difference between us and the Kauravas if we do the same!"

***Arjuna said: Yadi maam aprateekaaram ashastram shastrapaanayah; Dhaartaraashtraa rane hanyus tanme kshemataram bhavet.***

***(If the sons of Dhritarashtra should slay me with their weapons in battle while I am unarmed and unwilling to fight, that would be better for me instead of having to kill them).***

"Having spoken thus to Krishna right in the middle of the battlefield, Arjuna has cast away his bow and arrows," Sanjaya informed Dhritarashtra. "He is sitting down on the seat of his chariot with his mind full of pain and sorrow. Arjuna is despondent and seems reluctant to fight with his brothers and relatives in this war."

*Thus, in the glorious Bhagavad Gita, the scripture of Yoga, the dialogue between Lord Krishna and Arjuna, ends the first discourse titled: Arjuna Vishad Yoga (The Despondency of Arjuna).*

Chapter Two

# Sankhya Yoga

(The Yoga of Knowledge)

## Summary of the Second Discourse

Sanjaya explained the plight of Arjuna to Dhritarashtra, who was agitated due to attachment and fear. "Arjuna is slumped in his chariot, despondent with troubled and tearful eyes," Sanjaya explained. "When Lord Krishna saw Arjuna's state, he rebuked him for his dejection that was caused because of attachment to his worldly possessions."

***Sri Bhagavaan Uvaacha: Kutastwaa kashmalam idam vishame samupasthitam; Anaaryajushtam aswargyam akeertikaram arjuna.***

***(How has this dejection crept into you in this hour of crisis, O Arjuna? This feeling which is more suited to non-Aryans, is unworthy of you and will close the gates of Heaven for you).***

"Do not yield to the forces of impotence as they do not suit a warrior like you. Stand up, shake off this faint-heartedness and fight your enemies! Such action is unworthy of a warrior!" Lord Krishna urged.

"How can I fight my elders like Bheeshma and Drona in battle?" Arjuna asked. "Instead of killing such respected elders, it is better to beg for alms. How can I enjoy this blood-stained luxury by killing my elders?"

After failing to convince Lord Krishna, Arjuna realised his helplessness and surrendered himself completely to the Lord, seeking His guidance to remove the conflict raging in his mind. Lord Krishna took pity on Arjuna and proceeded to enlighten him.

"Arjuna, you grieve for those who are unworthy of your grief," he said. "The wise grieve neither for the dead nor the living. Even though the body dies, the Atman or the soul is imperishable and there is no past, present and future for it. Just like this body, the soul passes through the stages of childhood, youth and old age. But the soul also passes into another body. You should not grieve as the Atman never dies. Instead, it transcends all the five elements and is unchanging and eternal. Even if the pot is broken, the ether that is within and without it cannot be destroyed. Similarly, if the bodies and all other objects perish, the eternal Self that pervades them cannot be destroyed. It is the living Truth.What changes must always be unreal. What is real is what is constant or permanent like the Atman, which is the only reality. As names and forms are constantly changing, they face decay and death. Hence, they are unreal and temporary. All of us experience conditions like pleasure and pain, and heat and cold. This is because of the contact of objects with our senses that carry the sensations through the nerves to our minds."

*Lord Krishna said: Yadaa samharate chaayam kurmo'ngaaneeva sarvashah; Indriyaaneendriyaarthebhyas tasya prajnaa pratishthitaa.*

***(Endure these senses bravely, O Arjuna! One should be able to withdraw the senses from the objects, just like the tortoise that withdraws all the limbs within its body. Only the one who has the capability to be balanced in both pleasure and pain alike is fit to be immortal).***

After explaining about the immortality of the soul, Lord Krishna tells Arjuna about the performance of action without the expectation of fruit," Sanjaya informed Dhritarashtra.

"O Arjuna," Krishna revealed. "A man should not be bothered about the fruit of his actions like profit and loss, victory and defeat. These are all in the hands of the Lord and a man should perform his actions with a balanced mind, calmly enduring opposites like heat and cold, and pleasure and pain. Arjuna, you must fight simply because it is your duty to fight, freeing yourself from the desires of acquiring the kingdom or preserving it."

"What are the characteristics of a man with a stable mind?" Arjuna asked.

"A man with a stable mind is called a *Sthitaprajna*. He has no desires at all," Lord Krishna replied. "This is because he has realised the Self and is content within. The abandonment of desires and the consciousness of the soul are experiences that happen simultaneously.

A stable-minded person is not affected by adversity and has neither fear nor anger. Taking things as they come, he does not have any likes or dislikes. He neither loves the world nor hates it. But he has perfect control of the senses. These senses are powerful and draw the mind outwards. What one must do is to turn one's gaze within and realise God who resides in the heart, instead of seeking him outside. The Yogi, who has achieved a stable mind, ignores all the sense objects and remains unmoved, thus living a life of eternal peace. This eternal Brahmic state removes all the delusions from the mind and even when the soul departs from the body it does not lose consciousness with the identity of Brahman. Just as a man casts away his old clothes to put on new ones, the soul casts off an old body to enter a new one. The Self is infinite and powerful. The sword cannot cut it, fire cannot burn it and the wind cannot

dry it. The law of Nature states that birth is inevitable for what is dead and death is inevitable to what is born. Therefore, one should not grieve for any creature, O Arjuna! Why should one grieve over the inevitable as death is certain for whoever is born, just like birth is certain for who that die? The physical body is made up of the combination of the five elements," Krishna explained further. "After death, the body disintegrates as all the five elements return to their original source, making it impossible for the body to be perceived now. The one who understands this nature of the body and human relationships will never grieve. The Self is not easy to understand. The one that sees, hears and speaks about the Self is a rare and wonderful man. In fact, he is one among thousands."

***Swadharmam api chaavekshya na vikampitum arhasi; Dharmyaaddhi yuddhaacchreyo'nyat kshatriyasya na vidyate.***

***(Lord Krishna asserted to Arjuna that for a Kshatriya like him, there was nothing higher than a righteous war like this one. So, having regard for his own duty, he should not waver).***

"Fight, O Arjuna!" Lord Krishna exclaimed, coaxing Arjuna to pick up his arms. "If a warrior dies for a righteous cause in battle, the gates of Heaven itself are thrown open for him. But if you refuse to fight in this righteous war by abandoning your duty, you shall incur sin. People will remember your everlasting dishonour, a fate worse than death itself. The great warriors will think that you have withdrawn from the battle out of fear, and those who thought highly of you will no longer think so. Your enemies who were afraid of your might will abuse you, calling you a coward! What could be more painful than that? If you are killed you will gain Heaven, and if you win, you shall enjoy the Earth. So, stand up, O son of Kunti, and fight!"

The following narration of Lord Krishna is the Yoga of equanimity or the doctrine of poise in action. If a person performs actions with the above mental attitude, he will not reap the fruits of such actions.

"I have taught you the wisdom concerning Sankhya," Lord Krishna said to Arjuna. "Now, hear about the wisdom concerning the Yoga with which you shall cast off the bonds of action and be protected from great fear. Performing Karma Yoga or selfless action brings about instant purification of the heart that leads to fearlessness. It is the unwise who lay stress on the ritualistic portion of the Vedas with their flowery speech to attain power and pleasure. Those addicted to pleasure and power move away from the goal of salvation, attained by meditation and Samadhi or the state of Superconsciousness. According to the Vedas, Nature is made up of three qualities or Gunas — Sattwa (purity, light and harmony), Rajas (passion, restlessness, motion) and Tamas (inertia, darkness). Make sure you remain in the quality of goodness in Sattwa, O Arjuna. Be free from the thought of acquiring and preserving and be established in the Self."

Lord Krishna further explained to Arjuna that the action performed with evenness of the mind is the Yoga of Knowledge. Action performed with the expectation of reward does not conform to the Yoga of Wisdom as the true

seeker does not seek fruits. When one seeks fruits, it leads to bondage and is the cause of birth and death. Man has to take rebirth to enjoy these fruits but enjoys salvation if he is free from desire.

"O Krishna, what is the description of the one who possesses steady wisdom and is merged in the Superconscious State?" Arjuna asked.

"A man who casts away all the desires of the mind and is satisfied in the Self by the Self is the one who possesses steady wisdom," Lord Krishna replied. "He does not chase pleasures, and is free from attachment, fear and anger. When a man thinks of objects, his attachment to them increases. Desire is born from attachment and anger rises from desire. The man who sheds all desires attains peace, and this is the state of being established in Brahma, O Partha."

*Thus, in the glorious Bhagavad Gita, the scripture of Yoga, the dialogue between Lord Krishna and Arjuna ends the second discourse titled: Sankhya Yoga (The Yoga of Knowledge).*

Chapter Three

# Karma Yoga

## (The Yoga of Action)

### Summary of the Third Discourse

***Arjuna Uvaacha: Jyaayasee chet karmanaste mataa buddhir janaardana; Tat kim karmani ghore maam niyojayasi keshava.***

***(O Krishna, if you think that knowledge is greater than action, why do you urge me to engage in action that is dreadful? Arjuna asked).***

"There is a two-fold path in this world," Lord Krishna replied. "The Sankhya or the Yoga of Knowledge I have already explained to you. The second path is the Karma Yoga or the Yoga of Action. Even if one has achieved oneness with the Eternal, action still has to be performed as per the qualities born out of one's basic nature. Man cannot enjoy respite from activity by non-performance of actions and neither can success be achieved by surrendering them. No one can remain inactive even for a moment, and perfection is possible only by engaging in all action as a divine offering, combined with a spirit of non-attachment and sacrifice. Only the man with a God-vision need not engage in action as he has attained everything that needs to be attained. However, a superior being performs actions for the good of the masses and the world. Action is needed for one who has attained perfection as well as for one who is striving for perfection."

Lord Krishna quoted the example of Janaka, the great sage-king, who continued to rule his kingdom even after realising God.

"Each person should do his duty according to his nature," he explained. "Performing the duty as suited to one's nature with the spirit of detachment leads one to perfection."

"Why does a man commit improper actions that cloud his very mind and drag him downwards?" Arjuna asked.

"Desire causes a man to lose his understanding and sense of judgement," Lord Krishna replied. "Then, he commits the wrong actions. Remember that desire is the main cause of all evil actions. If desire is removed, one enjoys total peace, bliss, light and freedom. One must bring the senses under control to ward off desire and sin. Just as fire is covered with smoke, a mirror by dust and the embryo is covered by the womb, similarly craving and desire engulf one's understanding and good sense. By overpowering the self, you overcome the enemy called desire.

Lord Krishna urged Arjuna to action again, "Perform the duty expected from you, O Arjuna. Action is superior to inaction and one cannot even maintain the body if inactive. Perform your actions for the sake of sacrifice, being free from all attachments. With this action of yours, you will nourish the gods themselves.

Be nourished by them in return to attain the highest good. Remember that beings arise from food, and food is produced from rain. Rain arises from sacrifice, and sacrifice is born because of action. Action comes from Brahma himself and Brahma rests in sacrifice."

***Lord Krishna said: Evam pravartitam chakram naanuvartayateeha yah; Aghaayur indriyaaraamo mogham paartha sa jeevati.***

***(The person who does not follow the wheel of life that revolves by studying the Vedas and performing the sacrifices that are prescribed there, and instead lives a sinful life full of sensual pleasures, has lived in vain, O Arjuna).***

"But the sage who rejoices in his own Self does not gain anything by performing any action," Lord Krishna continued. "Neither can any harm befall him for inaction. Look at me, Arjuna! There is nothing in the three worlds that I should do. I have nothing to attain that lies unattained. Yet, I engage myself in action! For if I do not do so, how will men follow the path and examples that I set for them? The three worlds would perish if I stopped performing action. Just as the unwise act because of the attachment to action, the wise should act without any attachment for the welfare of the world. But at the same time, the wise man of perfect knowledge should not unsettle a foolish man who has imperfect knowledge. O Arjuna, surrender all actions to me with the thought that all actions are performed for the sake of the Lord only!"

*Thus, in the glorious Bhagavad Gita, the scripture of Yoga, the dialogue between Lord Krishna and Arjuna, ends the third discourse titled: KarmaYoga (The Yoga of Action).*

Chapter Four

# Jnyana Karma Sannyasa Yoga

## (The Yoga of Renunciation of Action through Knowledge)

## Summary of the Fourth Discourse

***Sri Bhagavaan Uvaacha: Imam vivaswate yogam proktavaan aham avyayam; Vivaswaan manave praaha manur ikshwaakave'braveet.***

***(I taught this Yoga to Vivasan (The Sun God) who passed it on to Manu. Manu taught it to Ikshvaku and the Yoga of Wisdom was handed down in regular succession).***

Lord Krishna revealed to Arjuna how he had taught the Yoga of Wisdom to the royal sages over the years. These royal sages were kings who also possessed divine knowledge.

"But after a long lapse of time, this Yoga has been lost now to mankind and has decayed. It is the supreme secret that I shall share with you today, O Arjuna, as you are my devotee and friend!" Lord Krishna declared.

"But you were born later than the Sun God," a confused Arjuna asked. "How did you teach this Yoga to him?"

"Many births of mine have passed, O Arjuna, as well as yours," Lord Krishna replied. "But I know them all and you do not.This is because I am born by my own Maya and yet I am unborn, being the Lord of all beings."

*Lord Krishna said: Yadaa yadaa hi dharmasya glaanir bhavati bhaarata; Abhyutthaanam adharmasya tadaatmaanam srijaamyaham.*

*(Whenever there is a decline of righteousness, O Arjuna, and the rise of unrighteousness, it is then that I manifest Myself).*

*Paritraanaaya saadhoonaam vinaashaaya cha dushkritaam; Dharma samsthaapanaarthaaya sambhavaami yuge yuge.*

*(I take birth in numerous incarnations from age to age to raise Mankind and join Man with the Supreme Being. I manifest myself whenever the world is dominated by unrighteousness and the dark forces assume power. I do so to destroy these dark forces and to establish peace and order in the world.I do so to establish virtue and delete vice from this world).*

"Adharma or unrighteousness drags a man down to worldliness," the Lord explained. "It is righteousness or Dharma that elevates a man and makes him achieve the goal of his life to attain liberation. The one who is aware of my divine birth and actions is not born again. Instead, he comes to me, O Arjuna! He is absorbed within Me, freed of desire, fear and anger and purified by knowledge and penance!"

Lord Krishna explained to Arjuna how he had created the fourfold caste in the world according to the differentiation of Guna and Karma.

"The four castes are Brahmin, Kshatriya, Vaishya and Shudra. The division has been done according to the Guna or quality and Karma or the kind of work," He said. "Both Guna and Karma determine the caste of a man. The qualities of Sattwa dominate in a Brahmin who has serenity, purity, self-restraint, straightforwardness and devotion. Rajas dominates in a Kshatriya who is blessed with prowess, splendour, firmness, dexterity, generosity and kingship. In a Vaishya, Rajas dominates and Tamas is subordinate to Rajas. He does the duty of ploughing, protection of cattle and trade. In a Shudra, Tamas dominates and Rajas is subordinate to the quality of Tamas. He renders service to the other three castes."

Lord Krishna then revealed to Arjuna the secrets of divine wisdom.

"One should seek divine wisdom at the feet of a liberated Guru," Lord Krishna explained. "Only a person who has realised the Absolute Truth can teach divine wisdom and such a person should be approached with great humility and devotion. God himself settles in the heart of the Guru and instructs the disciple. Divine wisdom can liberate even the most sinful person. When a person gains the knowledge of the Self, the fire and energy of that positive knowledge burns all previous actions with their results."

Lord Krishna gave the example of fuel which is burnt by fire. He told Arjuna that one must have undying faith and devotion in the quest to attain divine wisdom.

"For someone who has spiritual aspirations, faith is the supreme guiding force," he stated. "The mind that doubts is always led astray from the right path. Being in possession of intellectual knowledge does not lead to salvation as it does not give you supreme peace and freedom. Only by achieving mastery over the senses, developing total self-control and faith and devotion does one attain true knowledge within. That is how one attains liberation. The doubting soul travels on the path to destruction. The one, who sees inaction in action and action in inaction is the wisest among men as he is a Yogi and performer of all actions. Some Yogis offer sacrifice to the gods which is also the performance of action.

"There are sacrifices made with wealth, austerity, Yoga and knowledge, and all of them remove sin when offered to the Brahma Eternal. But wisdom-sacrifice is better than the sacrifice of wealth and other things. This is because every perfect action concludes in wisdom. You can cross the sea of sins on this raft of wisdom alone."

Lord Krishna cited the example of a well-lit fire that reduces fuel to ashes. Similarly, he said, the fire of wisdom reduces all action to ashes.

"Wisdom is the greatest purifier," Lord Krishna stated. "Actions do not bind someone whose actions are dedicated to Yoga and whose doubts are erased by wisdom. So cut away all your doubts and ignorance with the sword of wisdom, and seek refuge in Yoga, O Arjuna. Stand up and fight!"

*Thus, in the glorious Bhagavad Gita, the scripture of Yoga, the dialogue between Lord Krishna and Arjuna, ends the fourth discourse titled: Jnyana Karma Sannyasa Yoga (The Yoga of Renunciation of Action through Knowledge).*

Chapter Five

# Karma Sannyasa Yoga

## (The Yoga of Action and Renunciation)

### Summary of the Fifth Discourse

Despite the clear instructions preached by Lord Krishna, Arjuna was still bewildered and in a state of confusion.

"My Lord, which of the two paths is superior?" Arjuna enquired. "Is it the path of action or the path of the renunciation of action?"

"Both these paths lead to the highest goal of the realisation of God, Arjuna," Lord Krishna replied. "The final realisation of the Atman or the soul is the aim of both these paths and there is no real difference between the two. But the path of the Yoga of Action is superior."

Lord Krishna explained to Arjuna further that perfection can only be attained and one can be established in the Atman only after the purification of the mind through selfless action.

"The Karma Yogi who is aware of the Atman and engages in action all the time knows that he is a mere spectator. He is armed with the knowledge that he does nothing," Lord Krishna revealed. "He dedicates all his actions to God and shuns all kinds of attachment, desires and the ego. The non-wisdom of his Self is destroyed by the wisdom he has gained, just like the brilliance of the Sun. Thus, he attains salvation and is never born on earth again."

*Lord Krishna said: Vidyaavinaya sampanne braahmane gavi hastini; Shuni chaiva shvapaake cha panditaah samadarshinah.*

***(Such a sage sees Brahman in everything. He sees the One Self in all beings and creatures - in a Brahmin blessed with learning and humility, in a cow, in an elephant, and even in a dog or in an outcaste. He treats all of them equally and is free from earthly feelings like happiness and grief having achieved eternal peace).***

"But keep in mind that a man does not become a Sannyasi just by giving up his actions on account of laziness, ignorance, family dispute, calamity or unemployment," Lord Krishna explained. "The true Sannyasi is the one who is free from any kind of attachment or aversion. The renunciation of objects is nothing. The renunciation of the ego and desires is what is desirable. It is the foolish and not the wise who say that knowledge and the Yoga of Action or the performance of action are different entities. The true Yogi looks for the fruits of both paths and the position that

is attained by the Sankhyas is reached by the Yogis as well. The true seeker is the one who sees Sankhya and Yoga as one entity. But O Arjuna, Yogaless renunciation is to achieve misery. The sage harmonised by Yoga reaches Brahman quickly."

*Lord Krishna said: Brahmanyaadhaaya karmaani sangam tyaktwaa karoti yah; Lipyate na sa paapena padmapatram ivaambhasaa.*

*(Lord Krishna explained to Arjuna that the one who was devoted to the path of action had a pure mind, had conquered the self, had subdued his senses and has realised that his Self is the Self in all beings is untainted even though he is engaged in action. Lord Krishna cited the example of a lotus leaf. Just like the lotus leaf is not tainted by water, the true Yogi is not tainted by sin).*

"These self-knowers are keen on the welfare of all creatures on this Earth," Lord Krishna said to Arjuna. "Totally liberated from desire and

wrath, subdued in mind and action, they shun all external contacts with the world. The liberation of their soul is their only goal through meditation and surrender of action.

Then, after knowing Me as the One to offer their sacrifices and penance as the Highest Lord in all the three worlds and He who loves every creature that is born, they find eternal peace."

*Thus, in the glorious Bhagavad Gita, the scripture of Yoga, the dialogue between Lord Krishna and Arjuna, ends the fifth discourse titled: Karma Sannyasa Yoga (The Yoga of Action and Renunciation).*

Chapter Six

# Dhyana Yoga

## (The Yoga of Meditation)

### Summary of the Sixth Discourse

Sri Krishna emphasised once again to Arjuna that the Yogi or Sannyasi is the one who has renounced the fruits of actions, but not the actions themselves. When one performs actions without an eye on the fruits that they may fetch, it leads to the purification of the mind. Lord Krishna eulogises Karma Yoga as it is a stepping stone to the Dhyan Yoga or the Yoga of Meditation.

"Only a purified mind can be made free from all desires," Lord Krishna explained. "Once the mind is purified, it can perform constant meditation on the Atman or the soul. It is desire that creates imagination or Sankalpa and this drives the soul straight to the field of action. Hence, in order to realise permanent freedom and peace of mind, one must renounce desires."

*Aarurukshormuneryogam karma kaaranamuchyate; Yogaaroodhasya tasyaiva shamah kaaranamuchyate.*

***(A sage who climbs the ladder of Yoga has to use action as the means. But the sage who has already attained Yoga, inaction is the means), the Lord explained.***

Lord Krishna stressed on the importance of the lower self being controlled by the higher Self.

"The self should raise the self instead of lowering it," he stated. "The self is the friend of the self as well as its enemy. One must control all the lower impulses of the body, mind and senses by the power of the higher Self. It is then that the higher Self becomes one's friend. The Yogi has total control of the body, mind and senses and is united with the Lord. He sees God in all beings and objects and to him, there is no difference between friend and foe, between gold and stone and even between the righteous and the unrighteous. This is because he is in perfect harmony."

Now, Lord Krishna gave Arjuna practical suggestions on how to practice meditation.

"In order to meditate, one should select a clean spot that is secluded where there is no chance of disturbance. The meditation seat should be arranged properly and should not be too high or too low. It should be made of a cloth, a skin and kusha grass, one kept over the other. One should sit in a posture that is comfortable, with the head, neck and spine erect but not tense. The purified mind should be fixed on the Atman by concentrating between the eyebrows or the tip of the nose while meditating. The Yogi should keep the mind and the body steady and controlled while meditating in solitude. One should be free from both hope and greed."

Lord Krishna also stressed on the practice of Brahmacharya being absolutely essential for the participant to succeed in meditation. He said that the conservation and transformation of the vital fluid into spiritual energy provides great power of concentration. One must be totally fearless to walk on the path of God as well and have total faith in God.

"One must lead a life of moderation, O Arjuna," Lord Krishna stated. "Daily habits like eating, sleeping and even recreation must be moderate as any extremes spoil the practice of meditation. Once the Yogi has attained perfect union with the Self, he can never drop into a state of ignorance or delusion nor does he crave for the pleasures of the senses. But the life of a Yogi is not for the one who eats too much or for someone who does not eat at all. Neither is it for someone who sleeps too much nor for someone who is always awake!"

Lord Krishna laid stress again on the concentration of the mind on the Atman. He compares it to be like the steady flame in a place that is devoid of wind.

***Lord Krishna said: Yathaa deepo nivaatastho nengate sopamaa smritaa; Yogino yatachittasya yunjato yogamaatmanah.***

***(Lord Krishna explained to Arjuna that just as a lamp placed in a windless spot does not flicker, such is the concentration of a Yogi of controlled mind, who practices Yoga in the Self or is absorbed in the Yoga of the Self. This is a beautiful***

***simile that Yogis often quote when they talk of concentration or one-pointedness of mind).***

"But My Lord, is it possible to engage the mind so steadily on the Higher Self?" Arjuna asked doubtfully. "The very nature of the mind is that of continuous restlessness after all."

"It is difficult but not impossible," Lord Krishna replied. "The means to succeed in this practice is by using Vairagya or dispassion and continuous effort."

“What happens to the person who fails to realise the Supreme Lord despite all his faith and sincerity?” Arjuna asked Lord Krishna. “What is his fate?”

“The accumulated powers of his Yogic practices will ensure that he is blessed with a better birth in the future even though he has not realised God in this lifetime,” Lord Krishna replied. “This will only ensure that the aspirant carries on his quest by performing his Yogic practices with greater effort and faith to finally realise God.”

Lord Krishna then explains the effect of oneness to Arjuna.

“O Arjuna, the one who sees Me everywhere and sees everything in Me, is never separated from Me. Neither am I separated from him. The one who is established in unity and worships Me, who lives in all beings, resides in Me whatever be his mode of living. The one who sees equality everywhere, in pleasure or in pain through the likeness of his own Self is considered to be the Yogi of the highest order.”

He who, through the likeness of the Self, O Arjuna, sees equality everywhere, be it pleasure or pain, he is regarded as the highest Yogi!

In conclusion, Lord Krishna said that the Yogi who has managed to attain union with the Supreme Lord is superior to the ascetics, to all the men of bookish knowledge as well as the men of action. That is because the rest of them have not travelled the path to transcend ignorance and be merged in the Self.

*Thus, in the glorious Bhagavad Gita, the scripture of Yoga, the dialogue between Lord Krishna and Arjuna, ends the sixth discourse titled: Dhyana Yoga (The Yoga of Meditation).*

Chapter Seven

# Jnyana Vijnyana Yoga

## (The Yoga of Wisdom and Realisation)

### Summary of the Seventh Discourse

Lord Krishna said to Arjuna that the Supreme God has to be realised with the mind attached to Him and by practising the Yoga reliant on Him. The Yogi who scales this peak of realising God has nothing more to know. By this, Lord Krishna also wanted to convey that if one sings the glories and attributes of the Lord, one automatically develops deep love and devotion for Him. Then the mind is always fixed on the Lord. Real devotion is nothing but intense love for the Lord, and when one has this it is easier to gain the knowledge of the Self.

"The complete union with the Lord is difficult to attain," Lord Krishna declared to Arjuna.

***Lord Krishna declared: Manushyaanaam sahasreshu kashchidyatati siddhaye; Yatataamapi siddhaanaam kashchinmaam vetti tattwatah.***

***(Among men, hardly one in a thousand strives for perfection by aspiring for this union. Even among the few that aspire to do so, very few actually reach the summit of spiritual realisation).***

Lord Krishna then explained to Arjuna His manifestations in the Universe and the power that guides them. He classified these manifestations as His lower and higher Prakritis.

"The lower Prakriti is made up of all the five elements and mind, ego and intellect," Lord Krishna explained to Arjuna. "The higher Prakriti, on the other hand, is the very life-element that upholds the entire Universe. It not only activates it but also causes its appearance and final dissolution. So, my two Prakritis are the wombs of all beings."

Lord Krishna explained further that whatever exists is nothing but Himself. "I am the cause of the Universe and all the things that are present in it. Like clusters of gems that hang on a string, everything is strung on Me. There is nothing that is Higher than me, O Arjuna. But yet, I transcend everything as the Actionless Self. I am the flavour in the water, O Arjuna! I am the light that beams in the moon and the Sun; I am the vital syllable Om in all the Vedas, sound in ether, and manliness in men."

***Lord Krishna said: Punyo gandhah prithivyaam cha tejashchaasmi vibhaavasau; Jeevanam sarvabhooteshu tapashchaasmi tapaswishu.***

***(I am the pure fragrance in Earth and the heat in fire, the life in all creatures; and the austerity in ascetics).***

"Know Me, O Arjuna, as the eternal seed of all beings. I am the intelligence of the intelligent and the splendour of the splendid objects! I am the strength of the strong devoid of desire and attachment and I am the desire unopposed to Dharma, O Arjuna!"The Lord declared. "I know the beings of the past, the present and the future, but no one knows Me! The beings that are pure, active and inert all originate from Me. They are in Me, yet I am not in them. The evil-doers and the deluded are the lowest of humans. They do not seek Me and their knowledge is destroyed

by illusion. So, they follow the ways of asuras. Nature or Prakriti is composed of three qualities or Gunas named Sattwa, Rajas and Tamas. These three qualities lead to the delusion of the soul and make it forget its true nature, which is oneness with God. This delusion is also called Maya, and only the Lord can remove this state."

Lord Krishna explained to Arjuna that this was the highest form of devotion that leads to the union of the soul with God in His static as well as dynamic Prakriti. But there are other inferior forms of devotion as well which were performed with motives in the minds of the devotees. These ranged from people in distress, seekers of divine wisdom, and seekers of wealth and prosperity. "But the devotee closest to my heart is the one who loves Me for the sake of love alone," Lord Krishna revealed. "The ones that are resolute in mind and have taken refuge in Me, who know Me as the knowledge of the elements on the physical plane, as the knowledge of Gods on the celestial or mental plane, and as the knowledge of sacrifice in the realm of sacrifice, they are not affected by death, O Arjuna!"

*Thus in the glorious Bhagavad Gita, the scripture of Yoga, the dialogue between Lord Krishna and Arjuna, ends the seventh discourse titled: Jnyana Vijnyana Yoga (The Yoga of Wisdom and Realisation)*

Chapter Eight

# Akshara Brahma Yoga

## (The Imperishable Brahma Yoga)

### Summary of the Eighth Discourse

Arjuna asked Lord Krishna the detailed meaning of the different philosophical terms mentioned by him in the previous discourse.

"What is the Brahman or the Supreme Being? What is the Karma that you refer to?" Arjuna asked, full of questions."What is the meaning that pertains to this spirit, the elements and the centre of all the things within the human body, O Krishna?"

"Beyond all things manifest and not, beyond all the names and forms, there is the Supreme Being also known as Brahman," the glorious Lord replied. "He is Adhibhuta, Adhidaivam and Adhiyajnam and resides in this body as the centre of all things, including the Self or the soul. Prakriti or Nature is the being that pertains to the elements. The actions of worship, prayer and sacrifice to the Gods with total faith and devotion lead to being blessed by the Lord. The way to reach the Divine Being and freeing oneself of the bondage of the cycle of life and death and the pain and suffering of

this mortal life is to remember the Lord at all times and in all places, even in the midst of one's daily activities. Such steady remembrance of God through regular prayers ensures that one is rooted to devotion even before departing from the body at the time of death. Thus, after departing from the body, he will travel beyond bondage and darkness to attain the realm of the Lord Himself."

Lord Krishna emphasised on the practice of self-control. He said that one must exercise great discipline over the senses and slowly be withdrawn from outside objects. The mind within should focus only on God by uttering Om or any other divine name. Such steady practice of daily worship easily attains the Lord.

"But what is that Brahman? Arjuna enquired. "What is Adhyatma? What is Karma, O best among all men? What is said to be Adhibhuta and Adhidaiva? Who and how is Adhiyajna present in the body? At the time of death, how will you be known by the one who has self- control?"

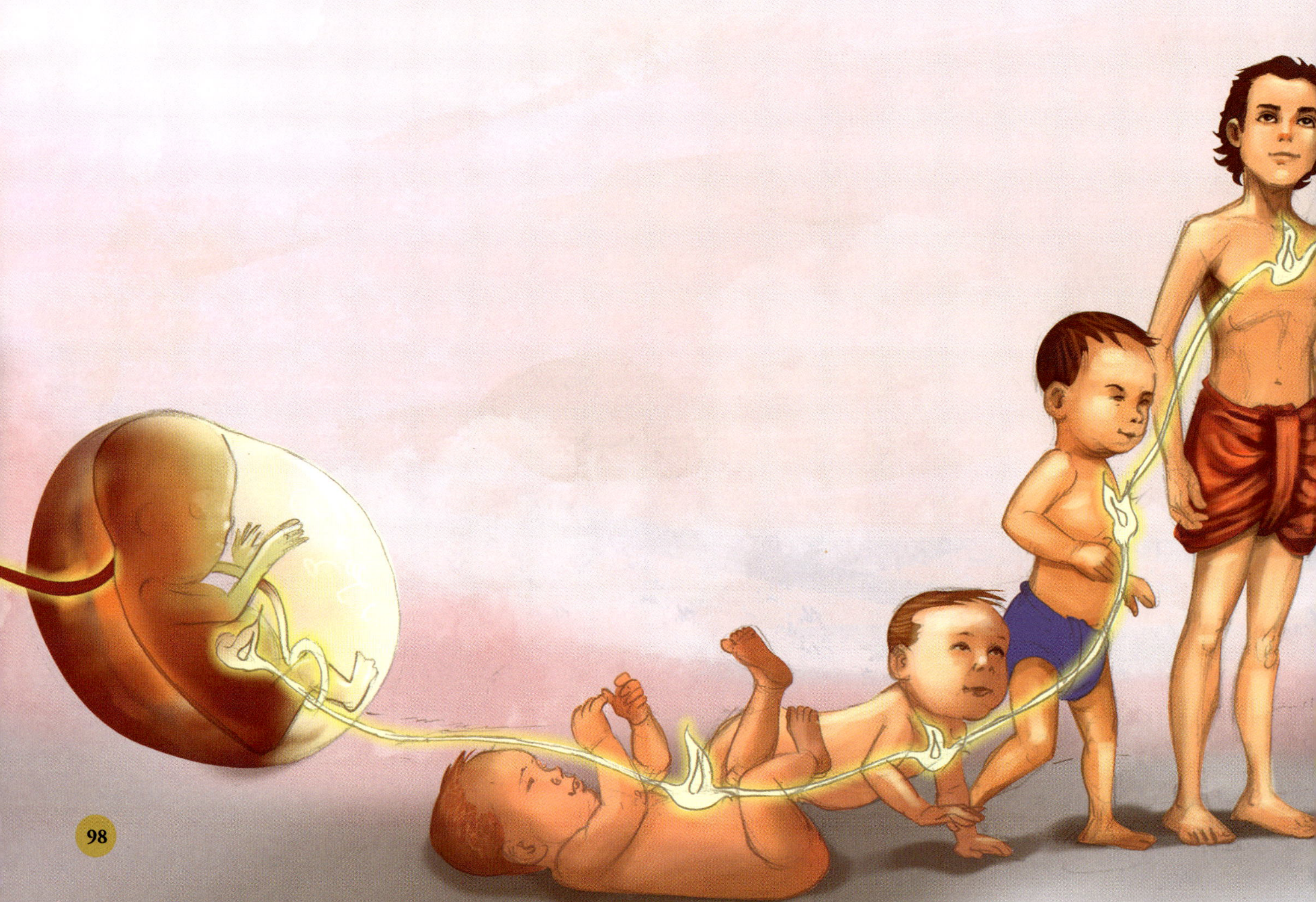

"Brahman is the Imperishable and this divine presence is embodied in living beings as the Jivatma or Adhyatma." Lord Krishna replied. "Self-knowledge is his essential nature. Karma or Action is the offering that is made to the Gods that causes the existence and the manifestation of beings and also brings about their sustenance. Adhibhuta is the knowledge of the elements and Adhidaiva is the Supreme Lord. Whoever remembers at the time of death as he is leaving the body attains My Being because of his constant thoughts about Me."

What Lord Krishna meant was that the most prominent thought of one's life occupies his mind during the time of his death. This very thought determines the nature of the body he would attain in his next birth.

"Therefore, remember Me at all times and fight Arjuna," Krishna urged. "If you have your mind and intellect fixed in Me, you shall come to Me alone! When the mind is not drawn towards any other thing and is made steady by following the method of habitual and constant meditation, one reaches the Supreme Person, O Arjuna!"

***Lord Krishna said: Avyaktaadvyaktayah sarvaah prabhavantyaharaagame; Raatryaagame praleeyante tatraivaavyaktasamjnake.***

***(Lord Krishna explained about the concepts of the coming of the 'day' and the coming of the 'night' to Arjuna. The first was the beginning of the creation of the world and the second was the beginning of the dissolution of the world).***

"The day of Brahma is of the duration of a thousand Yugas or ages, O Arjuna," Lord Krishna explained. "The night of Brahma also has the same duration. From the unmanifested state all the worlds are manifested to begin at the coming of Brahma's day. At the coming of the night, they dissolve and become unmanifested again. But there exists the unmanifested Eternal that is higher than all the unmanifested beings. When these beings are destroyed, the unmanifested Eternal is not destroyed and never ceases to exist."

The Unmanifested Eternal Being referred to by Lord Krishna is none other than the Para Brahman which is separate from the unmanifested form of primordial Nature. Being the cause of the unmanifested Nature as well as the Creative Intelligence, this is superior to them and is not destroyed when all beings are. As it is imperishable, this unmanifested Eternal is also called the Imperishable or the Supreme Goal. People who attain this Supreme Goal never return to Earth to be reborn.

***Shuklakrishne gatee hyete jagatah shaashwate mate; Ekayaa yaatyanaavrittim anyayaa'vartate punah.***

***(The bright path is the path taken by the true devotees to reach God. The dark path is taken by those devotees who perform sacrifices or engage in charitable acts with the expectation of fruits or rewards. The person that travels by the bright path does not have to return to Earth again. But the traveller of the dark path is reborn on Earth).***

"The Yogi faces no delusion once he is aware of these two paths, O Arjuna," Lord Krishna revealed. "Hence, be attached to Yoga at all times."

*Thus in the glorious Bhagavad Gita, the scripture of Yoga, the dialogue between Lord Krishna and Arjuna, ends the eighth discourse titled: Akshara Brahma Yoga (The Imperishable Brahma Yoga)*

Chapter Nine

# Rajvidya Rajguhya Yoga

## (The Yoga of Sovereign Mystery)

### Summary of the Ninth Discourse

Lord Krishna observed that Arjuna was a qualified aspirant to seek union with God and was full of faith and devotion. Hence, he decided to share the sovereign knowledge and the sovereign secret with Arjuna that could only be known by direct experience. Lord Krishna added that without faith in this knowledge, it became useless and Man failed in his quest to reach God and was reborn on Earth to suffer.

"Let me reveal to you the greatest secret, the knowledge combined with experience. Once you have known this, O Arjuna, you shall be free from all evil," Lord Krishna declared. "This is the kingly science and the kingly secret that is gained by direct knowledge and according to one's righteousness."

Then, Lord Krishna described His nature as the eternal, all-comprehensive Truth.

"I am everything that is visible and invisible. I pervade everything that exists. I create and sustain everything, and when the final dissolution of the world happens, it is I who absorbs everything into Myself. I manifest them again at the beginning of the next creation. The beings who are ignorant of this knowledge are trapped helplessly in the endless cycle of birth and death. As the Universe is created, preserved and destroyed, I stand as a silent witness, unaffected by anything and unattached to nothing. I am the sole director, preserver and supervisor of My Cosmic Prakriti. The ignorant beings who fail to recognise Me have an asura-like nature even though they are in their human forms. But the Yogi who has realised God, is a man of complete knowledge and sees Me in all living beings. Under my watchful eyes, Nature produces the moving and the unmoving, and O Arjuna, because of this the world revolves!"

Lord Krishna cited the example of the mighty wind that moves everywhere in the Three Worlds. But this mighty wind always rests in the ether. In the same way, all beings rest in the Lord.

"Fools who do not have discrimination despise Me," Lord Krishna declared. "Just because I have taken this human form, these fools have no knowledge of My Higher Being. They know not that I am the Supreme Lord. But the great souls know this and worship me with single-minded devotion."

Lord Krishna emphasised that his protection is assured to whoever takes refuge in Him. Regardless of the path followed by a devotee, he ultimately reaches the Lord. Although there are several methods of spiritual practice, the goal behind them all is the same. Lord Krishna said that devotion is the very essence of all forms of spiritual discipline. Devotion is the supreme element and the presence of devotion eventually releases the devotee of all bondage. But it is the Lord that monitors the degree and the motive of the devotion.

***Lord Krishna said: Aham kraturaham yajnah swadhaa'hamahamaushadham; Mantro'hamahamevaajyam ahamagniraham hutam.***

***("I am the Kratu, the Yajna, the Mantra as well as the sacrifice offered to the Gods," Lord Krishna revealed to Arjuna. "I am the medicinal herbs in the plants as well as the plants themselves. I am also the ghee or the melted butter. I am the fire and the oblation in the yajna).***

"I am the Father as well as the Mother of this world! I dispense the fruits of the actions of men and women. I am the One to be realised. I am the sacred monosyllable known as Om and I am also the Vedas. I am the goal, the support, the Lord, the witness, the abode, the shelter, the friend, the origin, the dissolution, the foundation, the treasure-house and the imperishable seed. I give heat as the mighty Sun and I also send down the rain. I am death but I am immortality too. I am both existence and non-existence, O Arjuna!"

Lord Krishna stated that even the man who is most sinful and evil manages to reach the Lord if he takes a sudden turn to follow the path of righteousness and repents for his actions. Regardless of the vocation one follows, the Lord can be attained if one has loving devotion and seeks earnestly. The most important thing is to fix one's mind totally on the Lord, dedicating everything to Him. This includes one's mind, body, actions, emotion and will.

"I accept anything as long as it is offered with purity of mind, faith, love and devotion," Lord Krishna revealed to Arjuna. "It may be a leaf, a flower, a fruit or even a little water. Whatever you do, whatever you eat, whatever you give or offer in sacrifice, whatever you practice as austerity, O Arjuna, do it as an offering to Me!"

What Lord Krishna wished to convey to Arjuna through this sermon was that the entire being of a man should be surrendered to the Lord without any kind of reservation. Only then would he experience a marvellous and miraculous transformation. Only then will he be blessed with the vision of God everywhere. As a result, all his sorrows and pain would disappear and his mind would be one with the Lord. He will be with the Lord and live his life for the Lord alone.

*Thus in the glorious Bhagavad Gita, the scripture of Yoga, the dialogue between Lord Krishna and Arjuna, ends the ninth discourse titled: Rajvidya Rajguhya Yoga (The Yoga of Sovereign Mystery).*

Chapter Ten

# Vibhuti Yoga

## (The Yoga of the Divine Glories)

### Summary of the Tenth Discourse

The all-compassionate Lord intended to encourage Arjuna to participate in the war and cheer him up. So, Lord Krishna decided to give Arjuna the instructions regarding the Yoga of the Divine Glories without Arjuna making a request for the same. Lord Krishna informed Arjuna that even the Gods and the extraordinary souls that were fully evolved failed to comprehend how He projected Himself as the Universe and all its manifestations.

"O Arjuna, neither the hosts of the Gods nor the great sages know My origin," Lord Krishna declared. "This is because I am the very source of all the gods and the great sages and there is no source for My own existence. The one among mortals who knows that I am unborn and without beginning and the great Lord of all the worlds is without delusion and liberated from all his sins."

***The Blessed Lord declared: Maharshayah sapta poorve chatwaaro manavastathaa; Madbhaavaa maanasaa jaataa yeshaam loka imaah prajaah.***

***(The seven great sages, the ancient four and also the Manus, received their great powers from Me because they had their minds fixed totally on Me. They were born from My mind and from them rose all the beings of this world).***

Lord Krishna also enlightened Arjuna that these living beings manifest various qualities according to their Karmas. All these qualities like truth, wisdom, and contentment to name a few, originate from the Lord Himself. The Lord absorbs his true devotees within Himself. These devotees have been bestowed the power of discrimination by the Lord because they have surrendered completely to him with their single-minded devotion. It is this power of discrimination that leads these devotees from the unreal to the real; and from darkness to light.

"O Arjuna," the Lord of All Things said, "Keep in mind that ignorance is removed and knowledge is gained through Divine Grace alone!"

"O Lord, you are the Supreme Brahman, the Supreme light, the Supreme Purifier, the Eternal and the Divine, the primeval God, the Unborn and Omnipresent," Arjuna exclaimed in wonder. "All the earthly sages have declared you to be so as well as the celestial sages like Narada, Asita, Devala and Vyasa. Now, you have revealed the same to me yourself! I believe all this that you are saying to me as true, O Krishna. But how is it that neither the Gods nor the demons know about your manifestations or origin? It is only You that knows Yourself fully, O Supreme Lord, O source of all beings, O Deva of Devas, O ruler of the world! Please enlighten me My Lord, by telling me your divine glories by which You exist, pervading all these worlds as no one else can tell me this but you. Share with me in detail, O Krishna, your Yogic and Cosmic power and glory by which you control the diverse forces of the Universe. I am not satisfied with your life-giving and nectar-like speech, O Krishna. I want to hear more!"

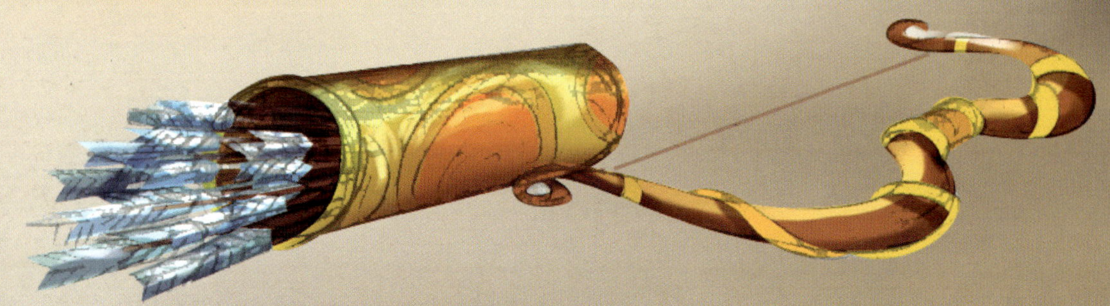

"Very well, Arjuna," Lord Krishna replied. "I shall now declare to you My divine glories in all their prominence. But they are infinite and there is no end to their detailed description."

The Lord then described His Divine glories, making Arjuna understand His limitless manifestations, and how He upholds everything in this world.

"O Arjuna, I am the Almighty Power that creates, sustains and destroys everything," Lord Krishna revealed. "I am the Self, seated in the hearts of all living beings! I am also the beginning, the middle and the end of all beings."

***Aadityaanaamaham vishnur jyotishaam raviramshumaan;***
***Mareechirmarutaamasmi nakshatraanaamaham shashee.***

***(I am Vishnu among the twelve Adityas, I am the radiant Sun among the luminaries, I am Marichi among the Maruts and I am the Moon among the stars)."***

"I am the Sama Veda among the Vedas and Vasava among the Devas. I am the mind among the senses and the very intelligence in living beings. I am Shankara among the Rudras, the Lord of Wealth Kubera among the Yakshas and Rakshasas, Pavaka or Fire among the Vasus, and I am the Meru among the seven mountains. The priests of kings know me to be their chief, Brihaspati. I am Skanda among the generals of the armed forces and I am the ocean among the lakes. I am Bhrigu among the great sages and I am the monosyllable Om among the divine words. I am the sacrifice of silent repetition among sacrifices and I am the Himalayas among all things immovable. I am the Peepul among the trees, Narada among the divine sages, Chitraratha among the Gandharvas, and Sage Kapila among the perfected. Know Me as Ucchaisravas, born of nectar among horses and as Airavata among lordly elephants. I am the king among men! I am the Vajra or the thunderbolt among weapons, the wish-fulfilling cow named Surabhi among cows and Vasuki among the serpents.

"I am also Kamadeva, the God of love among lovers. I am known as Ananta among the Nagas, Varuna among the water deities, Yama among the governors and Aryaman among the manes. I am Prahlad among the demons and I am Time among the reckoners. Among beasts, I am their king and I am Garuda among the birds. I am the wind among the purifiers, Rama among the warriors, the shark among the fishes, and Ganga among the rivers. I am the beginning, the middle and also the end! I am the science of the Self among the sciences and the logic among controversialists, O Arjuna! I am the first letter 'Á' among the letters of the alphabet and I am the dual among the compounds. I have faces in every direction and I am the dispenser of the fruits of action. I am also the all-devouring death and the prosperity of the prosperous. Among the feminine qualities, I am fame, prosperity, speech, memory, intelligence, firmness and forgiveness."

"I am the Gayatri among the mantras, the Brihatsaman among the hymns, Margasirsa among the months, and the flowery season among the seasons. I am the splendour of the splendid and the power in the powerful. I am victory! I am the determination of those that are determined and I am effort in those who make that effort. I am the goodness of the good! I am Vasudeva among Vrishnis and I am Arjuna among the Pandavas. Among the sages I am Vyasa and I am Usana among poets. I am the sceptre among the punishers, I am statesmanship among those that seek victory, I am silence among the secrets and knowledge among the Knowers. I am whatever is the seed of all beings, O Arjuna, I am also that. There is no being, moving or unmoving that can exist without Me!"

Lord Krishna explained to Arjuna that he was the primeval seed from which all creation has come into existence and that he was the Creator and the Soul of everything.

"There is simply no end to My divine glories, O Arjuna," Lord Krishna concluded. "This is but a brief statement by Me of the particulars of My divine glories! But what use is the knowledge of all these details to you, O Arjuna? Know just this that I exist, supporting this whole Universe by one part of Myself."

*Thus in the glorious Bhagavad Gita, the scripture of Yoga, the dialogue between Lord Krishna and Arjuna, ends the tenth discourse titled: Vibhuti Yoga (The Yoga of the Divine Glories).*

## Chapter Eleven

# Vishvaroopa Darshan Yoga

## (The Vision of the Divine Form)

### Summary of the Eleventh Discourse

After Arjuna's doubts had been removed by Lord Krishna by giving him a clear and detailed description of the nature of the Atman and the origin and dissolution of all things created by the Lord, Arjuna was ready to behold the Cosmic Vision. "O Krishna, by your explanation about the highest secret regarding the Self, which you have revealed out of compassion towards me, my delusion has disappeared," Arjuna stated. "I have also heard about the origin of the species and their destruction from you, O lotus-eyed Lord. I have also heard about your untiring greatness! Now, I wish to see Your Divine Form just the way you have described it, My Lord!" Arjuna requested.

"Behold, O Arjuna," Lord Krishna smiled and granted his friend and devotee's request. "Behold my forms by the hundreds and thousands. Behold these forms of different sorts, divine and of various colours and shapes! Behold the Adityas, the Vasus, the Rudras, the two Asvins and also the Maruts. Behold these many wonders that have never been seen before, O Arjuna! Behold My body with the entire Universe centred around it and within. See the moving and the unmoving and see whatever else that you desire to see!"

***Lord Krishna said: Na tu maam shakyase drashtum anenaiva swachakshushaa; Divyam dadaami te chakshuh pashya me yogamaishwaram.***

***(As you won't be able to see My Divine Form with your own eyes, I hereby give you the divine eye! Behold my lordly Yoga).***

Lord Krishna granted the divine eye or divine sight to Arjuna to witness His Cosmic Form which was invisible to the human eye. This experience

should not be confused with seeing something through the physical eyes or through the mind. This was an inner divine experience that could only be attained through intense devotion and concentration to the Lord.

In the meanwhile, Sanjaya was narrating the happenings of Kurukshetra to his blind king Dhritarashtra.Sanjaya said, “Having thus spoken to Arjuna, O king, the great Lord of Yoga, Shri Krishna displayed to Arjuna His Supreme form as the Lord!”

As Sanjaya had received the divine boon of witnessing the happenings on the battlefield of Kurukshetra so that he could relay them to the blind king Dhritarashtra, even he had the privilege of witnessing the Supreme Form of Lord Krishna and was among the chosen few who had witnessed this

divine form. “Lord Krishna’s form has several mouths and eyes, and comes with so many wonderful sights, O king,” a spellbound Sanjaya declared to Dhritarashtra. “There are many divine ornaments, garlands and apparel that He adorns and He holds numerous divine weapons in His many hands. The all-wonderful, endless and resplendent Form of the Lord has faces on all sides. If one had to describe the splendour of this mighty Being, all one can say is that it is like witnessing the splendour of a thousand suns that are blazing forth simultaneously in the sky.”

In the body of the God of gods, Arjuna saw the whole Universe resting, divided and sub-divided into its many groups. Lord Krishna granted Arjuna the divine sight thanks to which Arjuna saw the Lord in his Vishwaroopa or as the vast Cosmic Manifestation. Arjuna was spellbound with wonder and devotion as he saw the Lord in each and every direction. Arjuna was speechless and mesmerised as all the created worlds, the beings, Gods, creatures and objects stood before him, revealed in all their splendour in the one gargantuan body of the Lord. Arjuna also witnessed that it was the Lord’s almighty power that was controlling this great cosmic drama after rolling it into motion and action. Arjuna realised that it was the Lord’s will alone that prevailed in all things and actions, both good and bad. Then, the Lord urged Arjuna to fight again, stating that Arjuna was only a cause to bring about the greater good of the destruction of his enemies that were the evil forces. Arjuna, spellbound and filled with wondrous joy and with his hair standing on end, bowed before the Lord humbly with folded hands.

"I behold all the Gods in your body, O Lord," he said. "I also see many classes of beings. I see Lord Brahma seated on the divine lotus, and I also see all the celestial sages and the divine serpents. I see your boundless form wherever my eyes turn, with numerous arms, mouths, stomachs and eyes. I do not see the beginning nor the middle and nor the end, O Lord of the Universe, O Cosmic Form! Instead, I see you in the possession of infinite power, with endless arms, the Sun and the Moon serving as your eyes. I see your brilliance everywhere as I see you armed with the diadem, the club and the discus. I find it very difficult to look at you as your Form blazes all around me like the burning fire of the Sun.

I see you as the Supreme Being, the Imperishable who is well worthy of knowing. You are the great treasure-house of this Universe and the ancient preserver of Eternal Dharma. I see that the entire space between the Earth and the heavens and everywhere else is taken up by you alone. O great-souled Being, the three worlds are shaking with fear at your wonderful yet terrible form. As the Gods worship you with joined palms, the sages praise you with hymns. I also see that some of the Devas and Demons are staring at you in great amazement. Having witnessed Your Cosmic Form that touches the sky with its sheer size and shines in so many brilliant colours, with mouths wide open and large, fiery eyes, I am terrified in my heart and can discover neither courage nor peace of mind, O Lord Vishnu! I see all the Kauravas along with Karna, Dronacharya and Bheeshma entering into your Mouths. It is a fearful sight to behold! Just as the rivers flow towards the ocean at great speed, these heroes among men are entering your flaming Mouths."

***Arjuna said:Yathaa pradeeptam jwalanam patangaa Vishanti naashaaya samriddhavegaah;***

*Tathaiva naashaaya vishanti lokaas*
*Tavaapi vaktraani samriddhavegaah.*

***(These creatures that hurriedly enter your Mouths resemble the moths that fly into a blazing fire to bring about their own destruction).***

When Arjuna saw all the warriors whom he had been reluctant to kill on the battlefield rushing to their end by entering the Lord's mouth, he understood that he should not worry about the inevitable as the Lord had already made up his mind to destroy them. "Tell me about this form of destruction of yours," Arjuna requested Lord Krishna."I am the mighty Time who is now engaged in the destruction of the worlds as you see it," Lord Krishna replied. "Even without you, O Arjuna, it is destined that none of the warriors who have gathered in the hostile army shall live. Therefore, stand up and fight to gather fame. Remove all your fear to conquer all your enemies in battle and enjoy the fruits of the kingdom. Your enemies have already been killed by Me and you are a mere instrument, O Arjuna."

"Salutations to you, O God of the Gods," Arjuna exclaimed. "Forgive me if I have unknowingly insulted you with words uttered out of love or carelessness, by regarding you as my friend, O Krishna! I was unknowing of your greatness so forgive the words spoken to you in jest. You are not only my Guru but also the greatest Guru as there is no one equal to you in the world. So I bow down to you by prostrating my body before you, begging for your forgiveness.

Just as a father forgives a son, a friend forgives his friend, and a lover forgives his beloved, please forgive me, My Lord!

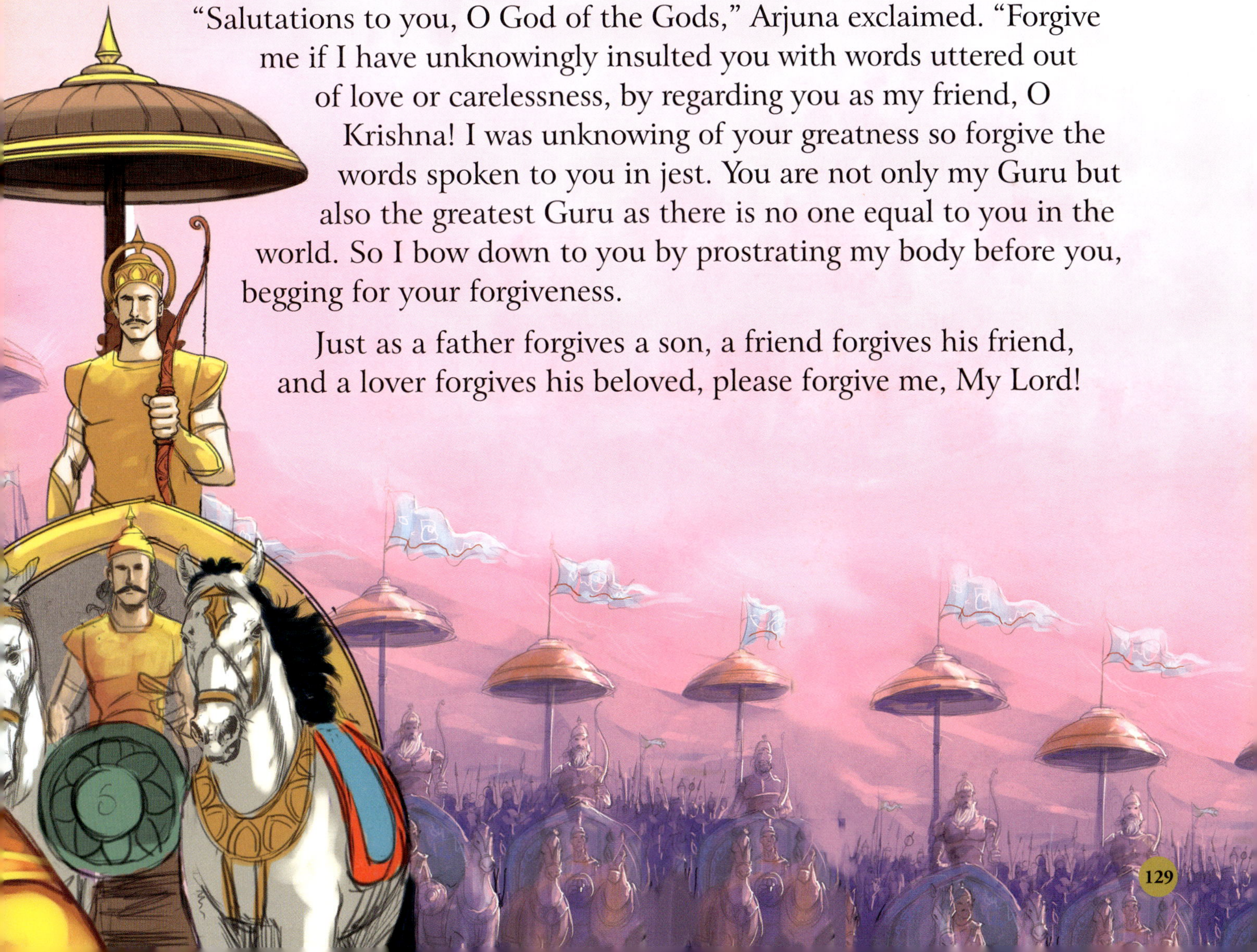

Although I am delighted to have seen this form that has never been seen before, my mind is still full of fear. Please assume your normal form again. Have mercy, O Lord of the Universe!"

Arjuna being a mortal was unable to withstand this Vishvaroopa of the Lord. He was unable to bear the sudden pressure of the expansion of consciousness and a strange fear gripped his soul. Lord Krishna then regained his original and gentle form and consoled the terrified Arjuna, who gained back his composure."It is very difficult to see this Form of Mine that you have witnessed, O Arjuna. Even the Gods are always eager to have a glimpse of this form. This vision cannot be experienced by any amount of austerities, sacrifices, study of the Vedas or acts of charity," Lord Krishna declared to Arjuna. "The only way that one can get access to my grand vision or Vishvaroopa is through supreme devotion. There is no other way, O Arjuna! He who is totally devoted to me and considers me as the supreme goal, casting off all other worldly attachments and is without enmity to any creature, he comes to me, O Pandava." Lord Krishna concluded.

**This is the essence of the entire teaching of the Bhagavad Gita, and this conversation summarises the entire philosophy of the Gita.**

*Thus in the glorious Bhagavad Gita, the scripture of Yoga, the dialogue between Lord Krishna and Arjuna, ends the eleventh discourse titled: Vishvaroopa Darshan Yoga (The Vision of the Divine Form).*

Chapter Twelve

# Bhakti Yoga

## (The Yoga of Devotion)

### Summary of the Twelfth Discourse

The twelfth discourse of Lord Krishna in the Bhagavad Gita emphasises on the fact that the path of devotion is easier than the path of knowledge in the attempt to attain God. Through the twelfth discourse, Lord Krishna revealed that Bhakti Yoga or the Yoga of Devotion is much easier than Jnana Yoga or the Yoga of Knowledge. Lord Krishna explained to Arjuna that in the Yoga of Devotion, the devotee worships the Lord in His Cosmic Form. But at the same time, he has a loving relationship with the Lord and remembers Him by chanting his glories and praying in His Name to attain union with the Lord.

On the other hand, the path of knowledge is more difficult than the path of devotion simply because here one is supposed to meditate on the formless Brahman. This is more difficult as one has to give up one's attachment to the body from the very beginning and be dispassionate towards worldly things.

"The devotees whose minds are set on the Unmanifested have greater trouble on their minds," Lord Krishna stated. "This is because the goal to attain the Unmanifested is a very difficult task for the embodied to reach."

By the embodied, Lord Krishna refers to those who identify themselves with their bodies. For those who are attached to their bodies, it is very difficult to reach the Imperishable Self simply because their minds are restless on account of their condition. These restless minds do not allow them to fix their minds totally on the Imperishable Self. When Arjuna asked Lord Krishna how devotion should be practiced, the Lord replied, "Those who set their minds on Me are saved from the ocean of the mortal Samsara. So, fix your entire mind towards Me, O Arjuna. Whenever your mind wanders, it should be brought back to Me. If you find this process of concentration difficult, O Arjuna, you should engage in the Yoga of Constant Practice by dedicating all your actions to Me. You should feel that it is My power alone that makes things happen and sets wheels in motion. If this mode of devotion also appears difficult, then offer all your actions to Me but abandon the desire for the fruits of those actions. Take complete refuge in me, O Arjuna as the devotee who surrenders to me attains perfect peace. Keep in mind that knowledge is better than practice, meditation is better than knowledge, and the renunciation of the fruits of actions are better than meditation. This is because renunciation is instantly followed by peace."

The Lord then described the qualities that a true devotee should possess. Neither does he have any attachment to anything nor is he averse to anything. He hates no creature and is friendly and kind to everyone. He possesses a balanced mind and is steady in meditation. No matter what the circumstances are, the happenings of the world do not disturb him.

He does not cause agitation to others by his behaviour and is self-controlled with a firm conviction. He is completely free from desire, joy, envy, fear, anxiety, attachment and egoism and just rejoices in the Lord within him.

***Lord Krishna declared:Samah shatrau cha mitre cha tathaa maanaapamaanayoh; Sheetoshnasukhaduhkheshu samah sangavivarjitah.***

***(The true devotee sees equality everywhere in the world, and behaves in the same way with friends and enemies. He is the same in honour and dishonour, in cold and in heat and in pleasure and pain, and he is free from attachment).***

Sorrow does not affect him in the least and praise and criticism is the same to him. He is not affected by fear and is balanced in both pleasure and pain. Having surrendered his entire being to the Lord, he is all forgiving, perfectly at peace and content.

Lord Krishna said that the devotee who is dear to Him does not rejoice when he attains desirable objects nor is he sad when he has to part with the objects that he cherishes. He also does not desire the unattained.

*Thus in the glorious Bhagavad Gita, the scripture of Yoga, the dialogue between Lord Krishna and Arjuna, ends the twelfth discourse titled: Bhakti Yoga (The Yoga of Devotion).*

Chapter Thirteen

# Kshetra Kshetrajna Vibhaga Yoga

## (The Yoga of Distinction Between the Body and Soul)

### Summary of the Thirteenth Discourse

This discourse has some of the most important, illuminating, inspirational and mystical parts of the Bhagavad Gita. Here, Lord Krishna gives us a lovely insight into the characteristics of the human being as an individual. This discourse is themed around the immortal soul along with its physical embodiment. Lord Krishna speaks about the metaphysics of man, the unknown.

"O Krishna, I wish to learn more about Nature or matter and the soul," Arjuna requested. "Please enlighten me about the body and the soul, about knowledge and that which should be known."

***Sri Bhagavaan Uvaacha: Idam shareeram kaunteya kshetramityabhidheeyate; Etadyo vetti tam praahuh kshetrajna iti tadvidah.***

***(It is this very body, O Arjuna that is called the Field. The person who is armed with this knowledge is known as the Knower of the Field by those that are already aware of this knowledge like the sages).***

"Know Me as the knower of the Field in all fields, O Arjuna! Also know that knowledge of both the Field and the Knower of the Field is true knowledge."

What Lord Krishna meant is that the highest and the best knowledge is the one that gives us divine wisdom and spiritual illumination to lead us to the divine state. The body is the Field in this exercise while the Immortal Soul that is Yourself that resides within the body is the Knower of the Field. Lord Krishna talks about the factors that make up the Field like the five elements, the ego, the mind, intellect and the ten organs. The great elements like Earth, water, fire, air and ether are great simply because they pervade all modifications of matter. The ten senses that Lord Krishna mentioned are the five organs of knowledge in the ears, skin, eyes, tongue and nose, and the five organs of action in the hands, feet, mouth, anus and generative organ.

The One is nothing but the mind. The five objects of the senses are sound, touch, sight, taste and smell. Lord Krishna declared that it is none other than the Supreme Being who has projected Himself and assumed the form of this Knower of the Field within this very body. That is the Self and that is the mystery of the individual soul that resides within the mortal body. It is this very thought or knowledge that forms the main subject matter in all the Hindu scriptures and the highest philosophical works. Next, Lord Krishna did a wonderful summing up of what true knowledge really is. He declared that the knowledge of the Supreme Soul is what grants us immortality. The all-pervading universal essence is the Supreme Reality that is present everywhere. Lord Krishna stated that this is everything! It is the one seer, the guide, the witness, the preserver, experiencer and the Lord of all things. The person who becomes aware of this mystery is no longer bound by activity even while he is living. Lord Krishna said that if one can gauge the difference between the Field or the body and the Knower of the Field that is the soul or the spirit, one can reach the Self easily.

For the modifications of change, growth, decay and death to take place, the birth of a man is imperative. The other changes of state only occur after the birth of the body. But in comparison, the Lord is birthless, changeless and deathless. A man is united with the Supreme only after he realises that all the manifold forms have their roots in the One just like the waves in the ocean and the rays of the Sun. Unity with the Supreme is achieved after the eye of intuition is opened by meditation and by the guidance of the scriptures and the Guru.

***Lord Krishna stated: Yathaa prakaashayatyekah kritsnam lokamimam ravih; Kshetram kshetree tathaa kritsnam prakaashayati bhaarata.***

***(Just as the one Sun illuminates the whole world, the Lord of the Field or the Supreme Self illuminates the entire Field).***

This is what this illuminating discourse intends to teach and impart.

*Thus in the glorious Bhagavad Gita, the scripture of Yoga, the dialogue between Lord Krishna and Arjuna, ends the thirteenth discourse titled: (Kshetra Kshetrajna Vibhaga Yoga (The Yoga of Distinction Between the Body and Soul).*

Chapter Fourteen

# Guna Traya Vibhaga Yoga

## (The Yoga of Distinction Between the Three Gunas)

### Summary of the Fourteenth Discourse

Through this discourse, the knowledge of the three cosmic qualities or Gunas has been shared by Lord Krishna. "I shall disclose to you the Supreme Knowledge, Arjuna," Lord Krishna declared. "It is the best of all knowledge and after knowing this, all the sages have reached the state of supreme perfection after their lives on earth. Those that have taken shelter in this knowledge with the aim of attaining a state of Union with Me are not born at the time of creation and are not disturbed when the world is destroyed. The vast Brahma is My womb and that is where I place the germ that leads to the birth of all creatures, O Arjuna."

***Sattwam sukhe sanjayati rajah karmani bhaarata;***
***Jnaanamaavritya tu tamah pramaade sanjayatyuta.***

***(Sattwa attaches to happiness, Rajas to action, O Arjuna, while Tamas, clouding knowledge, attaches to heedlessness only).***

Lord Krishna explained that these three cosmic qualities or Gunas were Sattwa, Rajas and Tamas or Goodness, Passion and Darkness respectively. By the precious knowledge of these three Gunas, each and every person can reach their goal of progress and happiness in their respective lives.

The secret of the success in worldly life as well as spiritual life is illustrated in the knowledge of the Gunas. This is because these three Gunas have the entire Universe along with all the creatures under their control. Lord Krishna explained that without this essential knowledge, one is bound by sorrow throughout his life.

"O Arjuna, it is these three Gunas that make up the Cosmic Nature," Lord Krishna explained. "The Cosmic Nature is the main source and the origin of the entire creation and all the things that live within it. So, everything is created according to their influence and irresistible power. The individual soul that is present within the body is no exception, and is also bound by these three Gunas composing the Cosmic Nature."

Lord Krishna further explained that the Supreme Being brings about the process of creation through the help of Nature that is also blessed with these threefold qualities or Gunas. "Sattwa or Goodness is the highest of the three qualities," Lord Krishna declared to Arjuna. "This Guna is the purest of all three and ushers in happiness, wisdom and illumination because it is bright, healthful and free from impurity. But it binds one by attachment to both pleasure and knowledge. The second Guna of Rajas or Passion is manifested by the thirst for great attachment and greed.

"This binds the embodied one by attachment to activity which in turn causes sorrow and suffering, O son of Kunti. The third Guna is named Tamas or Darkness. This is the worst quality and rises because of ignorance and leads to delusion, lethargy and darkness. While Goodness gives rise to pleasure, and Passion develops into action, Darkness only leads to error by clouding reason.

Goodness appears by overcoming both Passion and Darkness." Passion emerges while overcoming Goodness and Darkness, and Darkness rises by overcoming Goodness and Passion. When the light of knowledge illuminates all the gates of the body, it leads to the increase of Goodness. In increased Passion, the signs are greed, flowing energy, the performance of actions and desire, O mighty Arjuna. Increased Darkness gives birth to idleness, a sense of gloom, error and confusion. During the state of increased Goodness, when the soul departs from the body, it travels straight away to the spotless wonders of the Divine Being. In a state of Passion, the soul is reborn among the lovers of action. But when one sinks in Darkness, he takes rebirth in the wombs of the deluded instead. Learn this that wisdom emerges from Goodness, greed from Passion, and non-wisdom, error and confusion rises from Darkness, O son of the Kurus.That is why they say that the fruit of good action is Sattwic and pure while the fruit of Rajas or Passion is pain, and ignorance is the fruit of Tamas or Darkness.

"We should strive to drive out Tamas or Darkness from our nature with all our effort, O Arjuna, as it gives birth to error, sloth and sleepiness," Lord Krishna insisted. "We should learn to control and master Rajas and after we have learnt to keep it in check, we should wisely divert the activities of Rajas towards activities that are good and beneficial in nature. Sattwa on the other hand, should be nurtured with care, developed and preserved so that it helps us to attain immortality. The sage who is realised is beyond all the three Gunas or qualities. This is because even though the Guna of Sattwa helps him in his quest to attain God, this quality will bind him if he is attached to it too much."

Lord Krishna asserted that the seeker should be well aware of the symptoms and the signs of the presence of the Gunas so that they have a better understanding of their subtle workings. Only by this is an uninterrupted and smooth progress achievable in all aspects of one's lives, both spiritual and secular. The three Gunas are present in all human beings and they are interdependent as none of them is free from the operation of any one of the other qualities. They are not constant as well. Sometimes Sattwa dominates and at other times Rajas or Tamas is the dominant quality.

"What are the marks of the one who has crossed over the three qualities, O Lord? What is his conduct and how does he go beyond these three qualities?" Arjuna enquired of Krishna.

"Whenever light, activity and delusion are present, O Arjuna, the person who does not dislike them and at the same time does not long for them when they are absent is the one who has crossed over these three qualities," Lord Krishna replied.

*Samaduhkhasukhah swasthah samaloshtaashmakaanchanah;*
*Tulyapriyaapriyo dheeras tulyanindaatma samstutih.*

*(The one who sits without worry and is unmoved by these qualities even when they are active is the One. He is the same in pleasure and pain and to him a clump of Earth is the same as gold. He treats his friends and foes in the same kind manner and he has the same reaction in criticism and praise).*

"He is the one who rises beyond all these three Gunas with the help of spiritual practices and becomes free from sorrow, birth, old age and death, thereby enjoying immortality," Lord Krishna declared. "He is the one who serves and joins Me, as I am the image of Brahma, the Immortal and the Immutable, of Righteousness Eternal, and of joy culminating into the One.

*Thus in the glorious Bhagavad Gita, the science of the Eternal, the scripture of Yoga, the dialogue between Lord Krishna and Arjuna, ends the fourteenth discourse titled: Guna Traya Vibhaga Yoga (The Yoga of Distinction Between the Three Gunas).*

Chapter Fifteen

# Purushottama Yoga

(The Yoga of the Supreme Spirit)

## Summary of the Fifteenth Discourse

This discourse is also called the "Purushottama Yoga" or the "Yoga of the Supreme Person". In this discourse, Lord Krishna revealed to Arjuna the secrets of the ultimate source of the visible great Universe which has given birth to so many things and creatures. Lord Krishna cited the example of a huge tree which bursts forth with all its roots, branches, trunk, twigs, leaves, flowers and fruits.

"Just like the great tree that springs from the Earth with its many attributes like the foliage and the spreading branches that support this tree itself and in which they are all rooted, the Supreme Being is similarly the source of all existence in the world, O great Pandava," Lord Krishna explained.

***Sri Bhagavaan Uvaacha: Oordhwamoolam adhahshaakham ashwattham praahuravyayam; Cchandaamsi yasya parnaani yastam veda sa vedavit.***

***(The wise, they speak of the indestructible Peepul tree. This tree has its root above and its branches below, and its leaves are the metres or hymns. The one who knows this tree is a knower of the Vedas).***

This reference of the tree is allegorically made by Lord Krishna to the Universe which is like an inverted tree whose roots lie in Para Brahman, whereas the branches and foliage of the tree are composed of all the factors and things that constitute the very tree or the Universe.

"The branches of this tree are spread both below and above, and are nourished by the qualities or the Gunas. Its buds are the sense objects and below, in the world of men, the roots stretch forth, giving birth to action. One does not perceive the form of this tree nor its end, origin, foundation or the place where it rests after one has successfully managed to cut off this firmly rooted tree with the powerful axe of non-attachment."

But Lord Krishna asserted that this tree is a very mysterious one indeed, and one that is difficult to comprehend as it is a part of The Lord's Maya. It is nothing but a brilliant, apparent appearance without having any reality. Lord Krishna stated that the one who had full comprehension of this Samsara tree is the one who goes beyond Maya. To be attached to this tree is to be fully caught up in it. The only way one can transcend this worldly life or Samsara is by choosing the weapons of non-attachment and dispassion. Only when one travels beyond this visible Samsara by attaining the status that is supreme as well as imperishable, does he ensure that he does not have to return to this never ending cycle of birth and death. Lord Krishna described to Arjuna the wonderful mystery about His Presence in this Universe and the supreme place He occupies in order to preserve everything in the Universe. It is a part of Himself that manifests here as the individual soul in each and every body while He Himself is the indwelling Oversoul who exists beyond the Self. He is the bright, shining light that is present in the sun, moon and fire. His presence can be found as the nourishing element in the earth. He is the inner witness of all beings. He is the Supreme Knower equipped with knowledge even beyond what the Vedas teach.

Even the Vedas acknowledge Him as the One with the Supreme knowledge. He is the resplendent divine being who is beyond both this perishable magnificent creation as well as the imperishable individual soul which is a part of His eternal essence. He is beyond perishable matter and superior to the imperishable soul that is clouded in Maya. Lord Krishna explained that after the goal of attaining the Supreme One is achieved, no one returns from there.

"Neither the Sun lights up the world there and nor does the moon or fire. After reaching there, one never returns to Earth. That is my supreme abode, O Arjuna!"

Lord Krishna explained that when the Lord enters a body and when he eventually leaves that body, he takes these away just as the wind carries away fragrances from the flowers. But the bewildered do not recognise the Lord in his human form, and only those with the eyes of true wisdom recognise Him.

"The splendour of the Sun that lights the entire Universe and the light that radiates from the moon and fire, O Arjuna, know that light and splendour to be Mine," Lord Krishna declared. "I support all the beings with My energy and become the watery moon. I nourish all the herbs and plants. By becoming the fire sheltered in the bodies of the living, I join with the incoming and outgoing currents to digest the four kinds of food."

***Sarvasya chaaham hridi sannivishto***

***Mattah smritir jnaanam apohanam cha; Vedaischa sarvairahameva vedyo***

***Vedaantakrid vedavid eva chaaham.***

***(I am seated in every one's heart. Memory, reason and belief originate from Me as well as their absence. I am the author of the Vedanta, and the knower of the Vedas which classify me as the highest Purusha or the Highest Presiding Being in the world).***

"I have taught you the most secret science, O Arjuna! Remember that after knowing this, a man becomes wise and all his duties are accomplished in life," the Lord concluded.

*Thus in the glorious Bhagavad Gita, the science of the Eternal, the scripture of Yoga, the dialogue between Lord Krishna and Arjuna, ends the fifteenth discourse titled: Purushottama Yoga (The Yoga of the Supreme Spirit).*

Chapter Sixteen

# Daivasura Sampada Vibhaga Yoga

(The Distinction between the Divine and the Demonic)

## Summary of the Sixteenth Discourse

This discourse is essential and enlightening for anyone who wishes to attain happiness, prosperity and the blessings of God. For seekers, it is particularly relevant for those who are looking to achieve their spiritual quest in life. In this discourse, Lord Krishna clearly pointed out the intimate bond between ethics and spirituality. The intimacy between leading a virtuous life and the realisation of God that leads to the liberation of the soul is also mentioned. Lord Krishna spoke about two sets of qualities that are totally opposite in nature. The first quality is the divine quality and the second quality is the non-divine or the demoniacal. Lord Krishna stressed on the fact that while one should cultivate the divine qualities that are present within, the demoniacal qualities should be completely rooted out.

Lord Krishna provided the answers to the questions that have been asked by seekers for centuries. *What is the kind of nature that one should develop? What is the right code of conduct that one has to follow? How should one live one's life and act in order to attain God and divine bliss?*

Lord Krishna answered these questions with perfect clarity. He explained that the divine qualities that are pure in nature are the catalysts to be blessed with peace and liberation. These qualities are fearlessness, purity of heart, steadfastness in Yoga and knowledge, charity, control of the senses, sacrifice, study of the scriptures, austerity, straightforwardness, harmlessness and truth.

Absence of anger, renunciation, peacefulness, absence of crookedness, compassion towards beings, non-covetousness, gentleness, modesty, absence of fickleness, vigour, forgiveness, fortitude, purity, absence of hatred and absence of pride are also divine qualities.

On the other hand, the demoniacal qualities bring about bondage. Spiritual progress as well as leading an honourable life becomes impossible without having purity, truth and good conduct. If one lacks these three qualities and does not have any faith in God or in the presence of a higher Reality that exists beyond this visible world, he is reduced to being a two-legged beast instead of being a man.

"The one who is born in a demoniacal state possesses hypocrisy, arrogance, self-conceit, harshness, anger and ignorance, O Arjuna!" Lord Krishna stated. "Do not worry, O Pandava, as you have been born with divine properties!"

As Arjuna appeared to be sad at this disclosure, Lord Krishna assured him that there was no cause for alarm on his part as he was born with the Sattwic qualities that led a man towards salvation. Lord Krishna then proceeded to explain the demoniacal qualities in a detailed manner.

***Pravrittim cha nivrittim cha janaa na viduraasuraah;***

***Na shaucham naapi chaachaaro na satyam teshu vidyate.***

***(The demoniacal are unaware about what to do and what they should refrain from doing. They lack purity, truth, as well as the right conduct).***

"Such a person who is in possession of demoniacal tendencies is reduced from being a man to a beast that develops an ugly character and performs cruel actions.

He sinks into the world of darkness thus becoming his own enemy and goes about to destroy his own happiness as well as the happiness of others, O Pandava," Lord Krishna declared. "The demoniacal like to think that this Universe is without truth, without the base of morality and without God.

Centred on lust, power, wealth, evil and greed, these dark forces and ruined souls of small intellects and fierce actions become the enemies of the world and threaten its very existence. They are caught in a vortex of countless cravings and desires to become enslaved in sensual pleasures, hypocrisy, pride and arrogance. Their lives end in misery and degradation as their pride and egoism lead to this worst of fates. For this very reason, a wise person who is seeking virtue must remove evil and vice from his system and plant the seeds of virtue instead."

***Trividham narakasyedam dwaaram naashanamaatmanah; Kaamah krodhastathaa lobhas tasmaadetat trayam tyajet.***

***There are three gates that lead to hell. These are the gates of passion, anger and greed, and should be avoided.***

"A person who is liberated from these three gates to darkness, O Arjuna, does what is good for him and thus achieves the Supreme goal!" Lord Krishna stated. He meant that when these three gates to hell are abandoned, the path to salvation is cleared for the devotee. He receives the august company

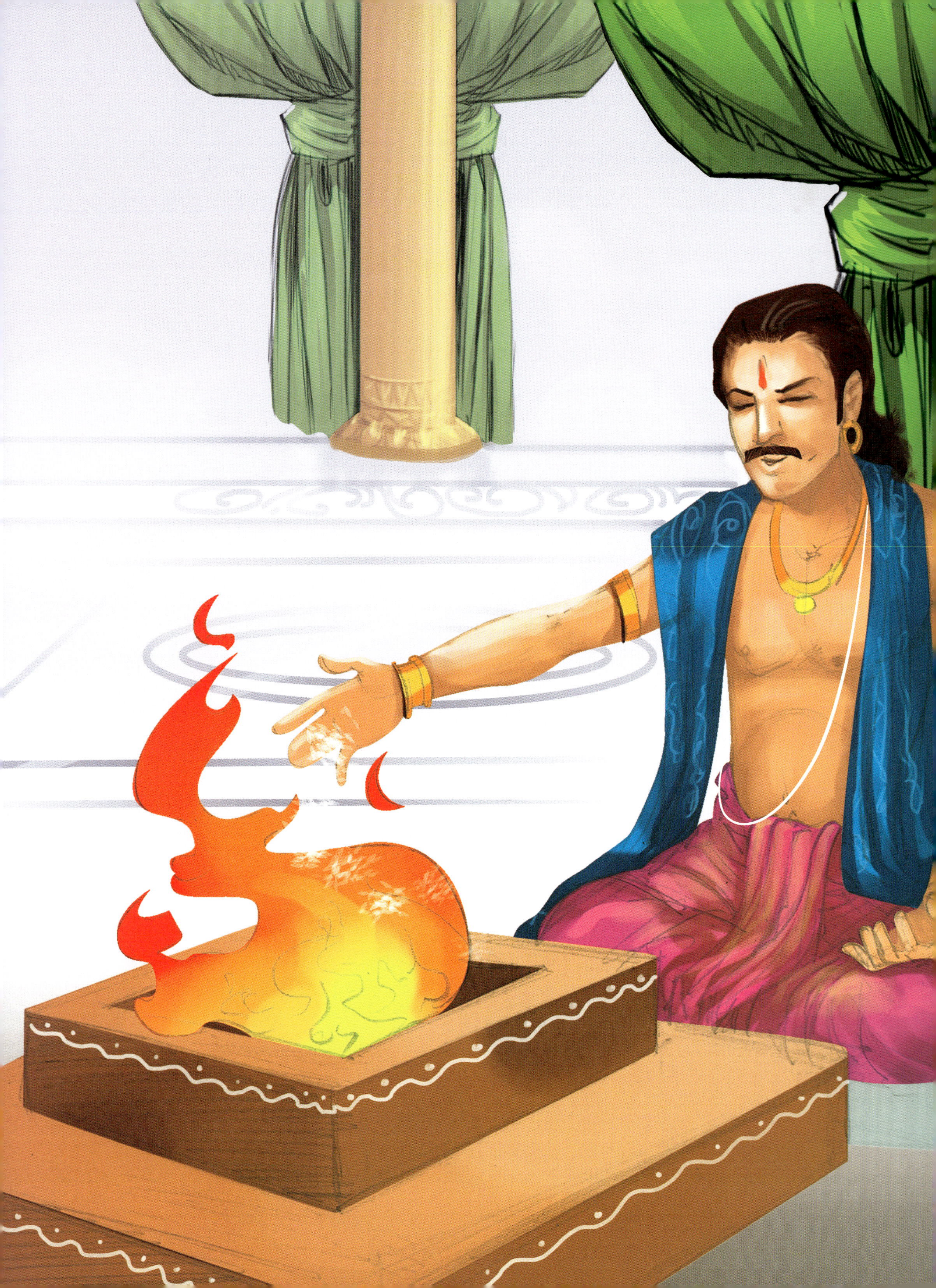

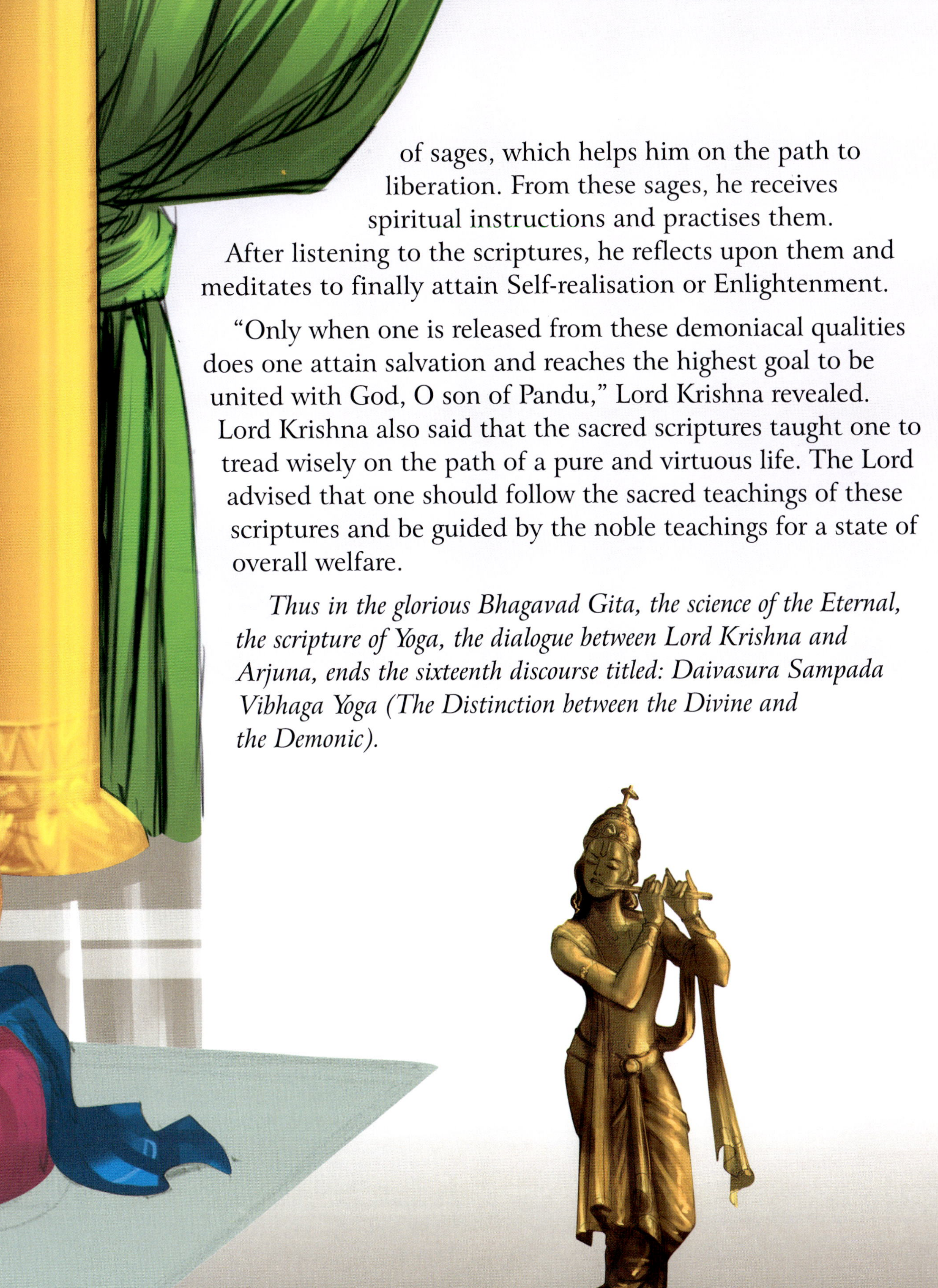

of sages, which helps him on the path to liberation. From these sages, he receives spiritual instructions and practises them. After listening to the scriptures, he reflects upon them and meditates to finally attain Self-realisation or Enlightenment.

"Only when one is released from these demoniacal qualities does one attain salvation and reaches the highest goal to be united with God, O son of Pandu," Lord Krishna revealed. Lord Krishna also said that the sacred scriptures taught one to tread wisely on the path of a pure and virtuous life. The Lord advised that one should follow the sacred teachings of these scriptures and be guided by the noble teachings for a state of overall welfare.

*Thus in the glorious Bhagavad Gita, the science of the Eternal, the scripture of Yoga, the dialogue between Lord Krishna and Arjuna, ends the sixteenth discourse titled: Daivasura Sampada Vibhaga Yoga (The Distinction between the Divine and the Demonic).*

Chapter Seventeen

# Shraddha Tarya Vibhaga Yoga

(The Yoga of the distinction the three types of Devotion)

## Summary of the Seventeenth Discourse

The theme of the seventeenth discourse originated with a question asked by Arjuna.

"O Keshava," Arjuna asked. "What is the position of those who reject the ordinances of the scriptures and perform their worship to God with faith? Is it Goodness, Passion, or Darkness?"

***Sri Bhagavaan Uvaacha: Trividhaa bhavati shraddhaa dehinaam saa swabhaavajaa; Saattwikee raajasee chaiva taamasee cheti taam shrinu.***

***(The nature of the faith of the Embodied one is threefold. It is good, passionate and dark).***

***Lord Krishna explained to Arjuna that the faith of men who ignored the instructions of the scriptures could be Sattwic, Rajasic or Tamasic based on the three qualities of Sattwa, Rajas and Tamas.***

He said that this would depend on the basic nature of the person himself. As is the kind of faith in a man, so develops his nature and this is in turn, is reflected in all the actions like worship, sacrifice, charity and penance. These activities produce results in accordance with the quality of the faith of the person. The acts that are performed with the right kind of faith lead to supreme blessedness. But a faithless task, on the other hand, renders the entire action to be barren and useless.

The Gods or the Devas are worshipped by the pure men or the Sattwic, Lord Krishna explained. "The Rajasic or the passionate indulge in the worship of the Yakshas and the Rakshasas whereas the deluded or the Tamasic worship the ghosts and the hosts of nature-spirits. The men of the world who engage in the practice of terrific austerities that are not recommended by the scriptures have the characteristics of hypocrisy and egoism within them and are driven towards darkness by the forces of attachment, lust, greed and vice. The demoniacal traits signify a meaningless torture of all the elements of the body along with Me who also resides in the body. The food that is so dear to every man is also threefold just like sacrifice, charity and austerity."

Lord Krishna explained thus that a man's taste for a particular kind of food was also determined by the Guna or quality that was existent in him.

***Aayuh sattwabalaarogya sukha preetivi vardhanaah;***

***Rasyaah snigdhaah sthiraa hridyaa aahaaraah saattwikapriyaah.***

***(The foods that increase strength, purity, health, joy and cheerfulness, and are good to taste, conducive to a long life and agreeable to the body are consumed by the Sattwic persons).***

The passionate like the food that is bitter, sour, excessively hot, pungent, dry and burning. This kind of food leads to pain, grief and disease. The food that is agreeable to the dark or the Tamasic is stale, tasteless, devoid of flavour, putrid, rotten. This kind of food is often rejected and cannot be served.

Lord Krishna declared that the sacrifice which is offered by the devotee without the desire for fruit or reward as instructed by the Holy Scriptures must also be performed with a faith that is firm and the belief that to do so is a duty. This is a Sattwic or pure sacrifice.

"The sacrifice that is offered with the intention of seeking a reward and for the acquisition of wealth is a Rajasic Yajna, O Arjuna," Lord Krishna explained. "A Tamasic sacrifice goes totally against the instructions of the scriptures. Here, there is no distribution of food and gifts among the poor and needy and there are no Mantras uttered for its success. This kind of sacrifice also lacks faith."

Lord Krishna also classified the austerities of the body as Brahma-conduct, the worship and reverence to the Gods, the twice-born, the teachers and the wise; purity, cleanliness, simplicity, straightforwardness, celibacy and harmlessness. The austerity of speech is the speech that causes no excitement when spoken and is truthful, honest, pleasant and helpful. The practice of the study of the Vedas is also austerity of speech. Mental austerity is nothing but serenity of mind, good-heartedness, purity of nature and self-control.

"This threefold austerity, O Pandava, which is practised by resolute men possessing the utmost faith and devotion and desiring no reward for their austerities, is termed Sattwic." Lord Krishna said. "But the austerity which is engaged in with the intention of gaining good reception, honour and worship and with hypocrisy is termed Rajasic. This austerity is short-lived and transitory. Tamasic austerity is practiced out of an idea that is foolish in nature. It could involve the torturing of the self or conducted with the purpose of ruining or destroying another person."

Lord Krishna also enlightened Arjuna about the classification of gifts according to the three Gunas or qualities.

"That gift which is given to one who does nothing in return, fully knowing that it is a duty to give to a worthy person, having regard to the fitness of place, time and the recipient, is thought good or Sattwic. The gift that is passionate or Rajasic is made with an intention of receiving something in return, or looking for a reward while making the gift, or given with reluctance. The gift that is granted to a person who is unworthy of the gift with unkindness, insult or contempt or without any respect is termed to be dark or Tamasic, O Arjuna," Lord Krishna stated. By the wrong place, Lord Krishna refers to a place that is not holy, where beggars and non-religious people gather, where the acquisition of wealth happens through means that are illegal such as theft or gambling and wealth is distributed among thieves, gamblers, fools, rogues and women of evil reputation. By the wrong time, he refers to a time that is not auspicious for the rendering of such an activity. However, this statement of the Lord does not discourage giving alms to the poor and needy.

***Om tatsaditi nirdesho brahmanas trividhah smritah; Braahmanaastena vedaashcha yajnaashcha vihitaah puraa.***

***(Lord Krishna describes 'Om Tat Sat' as the triple designation of Brahman by which were created the Brahmanas, the Vedas and the sacrifices. Hence, by uttering the holy 'Om', the acts of gifts, sacrifice and austerity as guided by the scriptures is always begun by the students of Brahman. The seekers of liberation who do not seek the fruits for their acts utter the word 'Tat' as sacrifice and austerity. The word 'Sat' is used to signify reality and goodness that is used for an auspicious act. Sat is also used for steadfastness in sacrifice, austerity and gift and the action connected with these to attain the Supreme).***

"O Arjuna," Lord Krishna declared. "Whatever is sacrificed, given or performed, and whatever austerity is engaged in without faith is termed as Asat! It amounts to nothing now, nor after death."

By this Lord Krishna meant that any sacrifice, austerity or charity that is made without being properly dedicated to the Lord is meaningless. It has no significance and will not help the doer achieve anything either in this earthly life or in the next life.

*Thus in the glorious Bhagavad Gita, the science of the Eternal, the scripture of Yoga, the dialogue between Lord Krishna and Arjuna, ends the seventeenth discourse titled: Shraddha Tarya Vibhaga Yoga (The Yoga of the distinction the three types of Devotion).*

Chapter Eighteen

# Moksha Sannyasa Yoga

## (The Yoga of Liberation by Renunciation)

### Summary of the Eighteenth Discourse

The eighteenth discourse of the Bhagavad Gita is the last discourse, being the fitting conclusion of the divine discourse of Lord Krishna. It is a broad summary of the foregoing portions of the Gita. However, it briefly captures the various important points that have been highlighted in the previous discourses. One beholds the final effect of Lord Krishna's lengthy sermon on Arjuna. The drama that had been created on the battlefield of Kurukshetra by Arjuna's sudden despondency and unwillingness to fight his kinsmen was finally resolved by Lord Krishna through patience, logic, reasoning and persuasion in these enlightening discourses.

The central message of all the discourses comes as an assurance that if one performs one's respective duties in life, one is eligible for the highest form of liberation. If one performs actions by eradicating attachment and egoism from the system and gives up all the desire for any form of personal gain, liberation is just a step away. If one regards the performance of one's duties as a form of worship that is being offered to God, His grace is achieved and one easily attains the Eternal One. Hence, this discourse has been aptly titled, 'The Yoga of Liberation by Renunciation'.

The discourse opens with a question posed by Arjuna to Lord Krishna."O Lord, what is true Sannyasa and what is true Tyaga (renunciation), O Keshava or Slayer of Kesi?" Arjuna asked.

"O Arjuna, real Sannyasa lies in the renunciation of selfish actions," Lord Krishna replied. "But more importantly, it lies in the renunciation of the desire or greed for the fruits of any action that one performs. The sages comprehend Sannyas to be the renunciation of action with desire and the wise know that abandoning the fruits of all actions is Tyaga."

***Tyaajyam doshavadityeke karma praahurmaneeshinah;***
***Yajnadaanatapah karma na tyaajyamiti chaapare.***

***(Some philosophers are of the opinion that all actions should be abandoned because they are evil while others declare that one should not abandon the acts of gift, sacrifice and austerity).***

"Hear from Me about the final truth about this renunciation, O best of the Bharatas. Learn that renunciation is known to be of three kinds. One should not renounce acts of sacrifice, gifts and austerity. They should be performed as they purify those that are already wise."

Lord Krishna stated that we should not renounce actions that are selfless and virtuous, and the ones that cause the welfare of others. But one must renounce every form of attachment and greed while engaging in such action and not expect any fruit by performing that action.

"Sattwic Tyaga or sacrifice is when one abandons attachment and selfishness while performing the duties that are assigned to him. This is true and proper renunciation as one neither hates unpleasant action nor is attached to pleasurable action."

The act of abandonment of attachment and selfishness while performing the duties assigned to a man is true and proper renunciation. This is also called Sattwic Tyaga or sacrifice where one neither hates unpleasant action nor is attached to action that is pleasurable. As it is not possible for one to renounce all action, one should attempt to renounce selfishness, egoism and attachment from the activity performed. Lord Krishna terms this as true renunciation and the one who has attained this inner renunciation, even Karma does not gather and bind him. The heart of the gospel of the Bhagavad Gita as well as the central message to its teachings is that God must be made the only object of one's life and this is the only means to one's welfare. Nature, as well as your own nature will urge you to perform actions. But when one abandons the idea of the fruits or rewards for the actions, no action will be binding.

Krishna told Arjuna about these five causes as stated in the Sankhya system that facilitate the accomplishment of all actions! They are the body, the doer, the various senses, the different functions of various sorts, and the presiding Deity. These five are the causes of whatever action a man performs with his body, speech or mind. The person whose understanding is untrained and who is wrong-notioned thinks of himself to be the sole actor when he is performing actions.

Lord Krishna also informed Arjuna that knowledge, the knowable and the knower form the threefold impulse to action while the organ, the action and the agent form the threefold basis of action."In the science of the Gunas explained in the Sankhya Yoga, knowledge, action and the actor are to be of only three kinds, O Arjuna," Lord Krishna reminded Arjuna. "When one sees the one imperishable nature in all beings, the undivided in the several, do know that this knowledge is Sattwic or pure or good. But the knowledge in which one sees all the beings of various entities as distinct from one another, know that knowledge to be Rajasic or passionate. Then, there is the trivial knowledge that clings to a singular effect as if it were the whole, without reason and any foundation in Truth. This is the dark or Tamasic knowledge."

***Niyatam sangarahitam araagadweshatah kritam; Aphalaprepsunaa karma yattat saattwikamuchyate.***

***(The action which is regulated and free of attachment and performed without hatred or love by one who is not desirous of any reward for the performance of the action, is known as Sattwic action).***

Lord Krishna explained that the person who is free from attachment and egoism, and is blessed with enthusiasm and firmness as well as unaffected by failure or success is a Sattwic or pure person. The Passionate or Rajasic are those who seek to get the rewards of their actions. They are cruel, greedy and impure and are affected by both joy and sorrow. The dark or Tamasic person is not steady, is sad, unbending, full of deceit, malicious, vulgar, indolent and procrastinating. "Now, listen to the threefold division of the intellect and firmness according to the qualities or the Gunas, O Arjuna!" Lord Krishna declared. "Sattwic is the intellect that is aware of the path of true work and renunciation. It knows what is to be done and what must not be done. It distinguishes rightly between fear and fearlessness, and between bondage and liberation, O Pandava! The Rajasic intellect is that by which one wrongly interprets both Dharma and Adharma, and fails to distinguish between what should be done and what should not be done."

By this, Lord Krishna meant that the scriptures contain what is known as Dharma or the righteous code of conduct in life, and Adharma which throws you into the dark abyss of ignorance. The Rajasic intellect fails to distinguish between the righteous and unrighteous actions.

***Lord Krishna said: Adharmam dharmamiti yaa manyate tamasaavritaa; Sarvaarthaan vipareetaamshcha buddhih saa paartha taamasee.***

***(The intellect that is covered in darkness, O Arjuna, and that which perceives Adharma to be Dharma and all things as perverted is called Tamasic).***

"Constancy of mind and body that is achieved by the unwavering firmness of Yoga, and which enhances the functions of the will, the mind, the life-forces and the senses is good or Sattwic. But the constancy that is fruit-seeking and is because of attachment and the desire for reward is Rajasic where the focus is on the enjoyment of pleasures and the acquisition of wealth. The constancy by which a stupid person does not shake off sleep, fear, conceit, grief, despondency and recklessness is Tamasic in nature," the Lord stated. Then, Lord Krishna urged Arjuna to listen to the explanation of the threefold pleasure, in which one rejoices by practice and achieves the end of pain. "This pleasure is like poison initially, O great Pandava," Lord Krishna declared. "But in the end, it becomes like nectar. This very pleasure is stated to be Sattwic that is born out of the purity of the mind after attaining the realisation of the Self. On the other hand, the second kind of pleasure appears to be like nectar initially, but later it feels like poison. It arises when the sense organs come into contact with the objects.

"This pleasure is Rajasic. The third pleasure springs from sleep, sloth and error and is always delusive to the Self. This self-confounding pleasure is called dark or Tamasic. O Arjuna, keep in mind that there is no being, either here on Earth or among the Gods in Heaven who has been liberated from these three qualities that Nature has given birth to. The duties have been distributed among the Brahmanas, Kshatriyas, Vaishyas and Shudras according to the qualities born of their own nature."

The nature-born functions of the Brahmin include the harmonising of the internal and external faculties as well as serenity, self-restraint, austerity, purity, forgiveness and also uprightness, knowledge, realisation and belief in God. Heroism, prowess, generosity, lordliness, splendour, firmness, dexterity and also not fleeing from battle are the duties of Kshatriyas, born of their own nature. The natural duties of the Vaishya or the merchant class are agriculture, cattle-rearing and trade. The action consisting of service is the natural duty of the Shudra."

The basic crux of this sermon of Lord Krishna emphasised on the point that a man's heart went through the process of purification and he attained

Heaven if he performed his duties in the right manner according to the order of life. "Each man when devoted to his own duty attains perfection, O Partha," Lord Krishna explained. "Listen as I disclose how he attains perfection while he is engaged in his own duty."

***Lord Krishna said: Yatah pravrittirbhootaanaam yena sarvamidam tatam; Swakarmanaa tamabhyarchya siddhim vindati maanavah.***

***(Man attains perfection and wins success because of the performance of his characteristic function. He worships Him from whom all beings have evolved and who pervades everything else).***

By this Lord Krishna meant that Man attains perfection by worshipping the Lord through the performance of his own duty. Thus, he becomes qualified for Self-knowledge.

The Blessed Lord told Arjuna that one's own characteristic duty when devoid of merits is still better than another's characteristic duty that is well performed. The one who performs the duty ordained by his own nature incurs no sin.

***Lord Krishna said: Sahajam karma kaunteya sadoshamapi na tyajet; Sarvaarambhaa hi doshena dhoomenaagnirivaavritaah.***

***(One should not abandon the duty to which one is born, O son of Kunti, even though faulty, because all undertakings are enveloped by evil just as fire is by smoke).***

***Lord Krishna said: Asaktabuddhih sarvatra jitaatmaa vigatasprihah; Naishkarmyasiddhim paramaam sannyaasenaadhigacchati.***

***(He who possesses an intellect that is attached everywhere, who has subdued his Self, and who has managed to rid himself of desire- He attains the supreme state of freedom from action by renunciation).***

"Learn from Me in brief how the one who has attained perfection reaches that supreme state of knowledge called Brahman," Lord Krishna declared to Arjuna. "He is equipped with an intellect that is pure, controls the self by firmness, abandons sound and the other sense-objects and overcomes likes

and dislikes. He lives in solitude, eating little food, has a subdued body and mind, and is always engaged in concentration and meditation, and fully rests on dispassionateness. He has shaken off egoism, strength, arrogance, anger, desire, and covetousness. He considers nothing to be his own and this tranquilised man is fit to be Brahma-natured. By becoming Brahman, serene in the Self, he neither grieves nor craves. He is the same to all beings and attains supreme devotion unto Me. By his devotion, he realises Me in truth, he knows what and who I am; and knowing Me in truth, he enters into the Supreme. By taking refuge in Me, he obtains the eternal, imperishable state or abode by My Grace. With his mind surrendering all actions unto Me, considering and revering me to be Supreme, he takes the help of this understanding by always fixing his mind on Me.

Having your mind settled on Me, you shall overcome all the obstacles in your path by My Grace. But if you do not listen because of egoism, you will perish. If, sheltered in egoism, you think: 'I will not fight', this resolve of yours will be in vain as Nature will compel you to fight! O Arjuna, bound by your own Karma that is born of your own nature, you have to perform that action that you now refuse to do blinded by your own delusion. You have to do that helplessly, even against your will!"

***Lord Krishna said: Eeshwarah sarvabhootaanaam hriddeshe'rjuna tishthati; Bhraamayan sarvabhootaani yantraaroodhaani maayayaa.***

***(The Lord dwells in the hearts of all beings, causing them to revolve as if they are mounted on a machine! The Lord does this by his Illusive Power).***

"Fly to The Lord for shelter with all your nature, O Bharata," Lord Krishna urged Arjuna. "By His Grace, you shall obtain supreme peace and the eternal abode.

I have declared to you wisdom that is more secret than secrecy itself. Consider this secret of secrets fully and then act as you deem fit, O brave Pandava!

Hear My supreme word again which is the best secret of them all. As you are extremely dear to Me, I shall speak for your good."

***Lord Krishna said: Manmanaa bhava madbhakto madyaajee maam namaskuru; Maamevaishyasi satyam te pratijaane priyo'si me.***

***(Fix your mind on Me, devote yourself to Me, sacrifice to Me, bow down to Me. Then, you shall come to me truly. I vow this to you as you are dear to Me).***

***Lord Krishna said: Sarvadharmaan parityajya maamekam sharanam vraja; Aham twaa sarvapaapebhyo mokshayishyaami maa shuchah.***

***(Abandon all duties, and take shelter in Me alone. Do not grieve as it is I who will liberate you from all sins).***

Lord Krishna said that this message was for Arjuna alone."This is not to be spoken to someone who does not perform austerities, to one who is not devoted, to the person who does not render service, who does not desire to listen or the one who dislikes me. The one who has supreme devotion towards Me and teaches this supreme secret to My devotees, shall come to Me without doubt. Nor shall be there among men any one doing a greater service to Him than him.

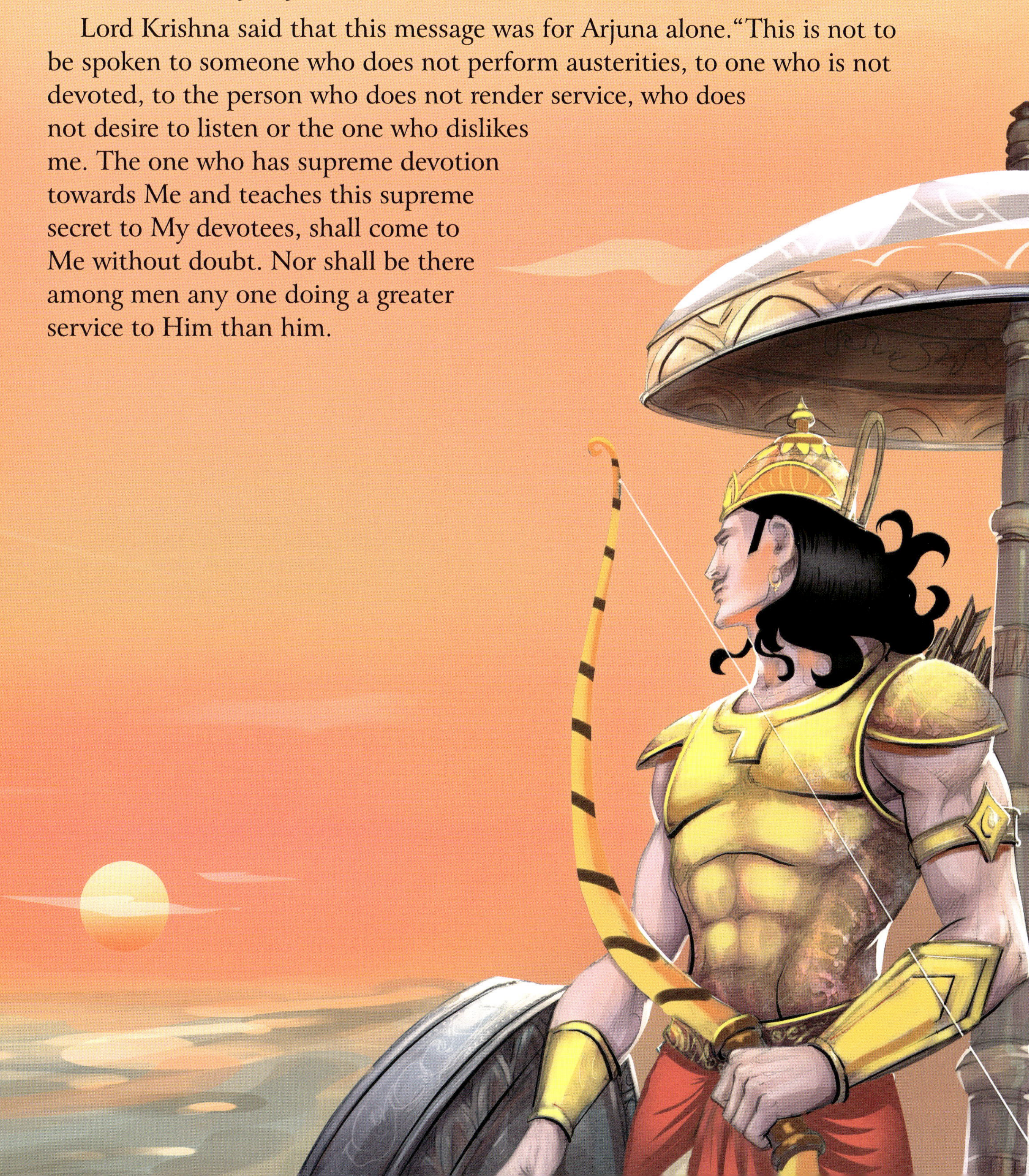

He shall also be extremely dear to Him than any other person on Earth. The one who shall study this sacred discourse and this dialogue will be destined to worship Me with wisdom-sacrifice. The man who hears this with full faith and freedom from dislike will be liberated as well and shall attain the world of those with righteous deeds. Have you, O Arjuna, listened to this with single-pointed attention? Has the delusion of your ignorance been fully destroyed, O great warrior?"

"O Krishna, my delusion has been completely destroyed as I have gained precious knowledge thanks to Your Grace," Arjuna replied gratefully. "My mind is firm now and all my doubts have disappeared. I shall do your bidding and fight!"

Sanjaya now concluded his narrative using his divine vision to the blind king Dhritarashtra that described the discourses of Lord Krishna to Arjuna before the great battle of Kurukshetra. "Thus, I have heard this wonderful dialogue between the great Lord Krishna and the high-souled Arjuna, and it has caused my hair to stand on end.Where there is such obedience as that of Arjuna," Sanjaya declared to Dhritarashtra, "and there is such willing readiness to carry out the divine teachings that the Lord has imparted to him, surely all prosperity, blessings, glory and victory will prevail on him."

***Sanjaya said:Vyaasaprasaadaacchrutavaan etadguhyamaham param;***
***Yogam yogeshwaraat krishnaat saakshaat kathayatah swayam.***

***(Through the Grace of Veda Vyasa, I am blessed to have heard this highest supreme secret directly from the mouth of Lord Krishna, the Lord of Yoga himself teaching in my presence).***

"O King," Sanjaya exclaimed to Dhritarashtra. "Recalling this marvellous and holy dialogue between Lord Krishna and Arjuna, I rejoice again and again! Also remembering repeatedly that most wonderful form of Hari, my wonder increases manifold, and I rejoice again and again! Wherever there is the presence of Krishna, the Lord of Yoga, and wherever there is Arjuna, the great archer, there is prosperity, happiness, victory and firm policy. That is my firm conviction."

***Hari Om Tat Sat***

***Iti Srimad Bhagavadgeetaasoopanishatsu Brahmavidyaayaam Yogashaastre Sri Krishnaarjunasamvaade Mokshasannyaasayogo Naama Ashtaadasho'dhyaayah***

*Thus in the Upanishads of the glorious Bhagavad Gita, the science of the Eternal, the scripture of Yoga, the dialogue between Lord Krishna and Arjuna, ends the eighteenth discourse titled: The Yoga of Liberation by Renunciation.*

***Om Shanti! Shanti! Shanti!***

# Gita Mahatmya

## The Glory of the Gita

**A dialogue between Lord Vishnu and the Earth**
**From the Varaha Purana**

(To be read at the end of the day's Gita study)

***Sri Ganeshaaya Namah! Gopaalakrishnaaya Namah!***

***Dharovaacha: Bhagavan parameshaana bhaktiravyabhichaarinee;***
***Praarabdham bhujyamaanasya katham bhavati he prabho.***

***(Earth asked the Supreme Lord: "How can unflinching devotion arise in one who is immersed in the karmas or actions of his daily life)?***

*Sri Vishnuruvaacha: Praarabdham bhujyamaano hi geetaabhyaasaratah sadaa; Sa muktah sa sukhee loke karmanaa nopalipyate.*

*(Lord Vishnu replied: By the engagement in the performance of the worldly duties, the one who is regular in the study of the Gita becomes free. He is the happiest man in this world as he is not bound by Karma).*

*Mahaapaapaadipaapaani geetaadhyaanam karoti chet; Kwachit sparsham na kurvanti nalineedalam ambuvat.*

*(Just like the water does not stain the lotus leaf, sins do not taint a person who recites the Gita regularly).*

*Geetaayaah pustakam yatra yatra paathah pravartate; Tatra sarvaani teerthaani prayaagaadeeni tatra vai.*

*(All the sacred places of pilgrimage like Prayag reside in that place where the Gita is kept, and where the Gita is read, said the Lord).*

*Sarve devaashcha rishayo yoginahpannagaashcha ye; Gopaalaa gopikaa vaapi naaradoddhava paarshadaih.*

*(All the gods, sages, yogins, divine serpents, the friends and devotees of Lord Krishna - the gopalas and the gopikas - Narada, Uddhava and others reside here as well).*

*Sahaayo jaayate sheeghram yatra geetaa pravartate;*

*Yatra geetaavichaarashcha pathanam paathanam shrutam; Tatraaham nishchitam prithvi nivasaami sadaiva hi.*

*(Lord Vishnu said: O Earth, Divine help arrives quickly wherever the Gita is recited. I live forever where it is read, heard, taught and discussed).*

*Geetaashraye'ham tishthaami geetaa me chottamam griham; Geetaajnaanam upaashritya treen Uokaan paalayaamyaham.*

*(I take refuge in the Gita, and the Gita is My best abode. I protect all the three worlds with the knowledge of the Gita).*

*Geetaa me paramaa vidyaa brahmaroopaa na samshayah; Ardhamaatraaksharaa nityaa swaanirvaachyapadaatmikaa.*

*(The Gita is My highest science, which is unquestioning about the form of Brahman, the Eternal, the Ardhamatra (of the Pranava Om), and the most extreme splendour of the Self).*

*Chidaanandena krishnena proktaa swamukhato'rjuna; Vedatrayee paraanandaa tatwaarthajnaanasamyutaa.*

*(The Gita was spoken by the blessed, the all-knowing Lord Krishna and this wisdom was imparted through His own mouth to Arjuna. The Gita has the very essence of the Vedas, which is the knowledge of the Reality and is full of supreme bliss).*

*Through this discourse, Lord Vishnu emphasises that the Gita contains the cream of the Vedas and Upanishads. So, this universal scripture is meant for people of all temperaments and all ages.*

*Yoashtaadasha japen nityam naro nishchalamaanasah; Jnaanasiddhim sa labhate tato yaati param padam.*

*(The one who recites the eighteen chapters of the Bhagavad Gita every day with a pure and steadfast mind attains perfection in knowledge to reach the highest state attainable to Man or the Supreme Goal of Unity with God).*

*Paathe'asamarthah sampoornam tato'rdham paathamaacharet; Tadaa godaanajam punyam labhate naatra samshayah.*

*(However, if a complete reading is not possible, and even if only half of the Gita is read, he attains the benefit of giving a cow as a gift. There is no doubt about this).*

*Tribhaagam pathamaanastu gangaasnaanaphalam labhet; Shadamsham japamaanastu somayaagaphalam labhet.*

*(The one who recited the one-third part of the Gita receives the merit that is equal to a bath in the sacred river Ganges. The one who recites one-sixth of the Gita attains the merit of the act of performing a Soma sacrifice).*

*Ekaadhyaayam tu yo nityam pathate bhaktisamyutah; Rudralokam avaapnoti gano bhootwaa vasecchiram.*

*(The person who reads one discourse of the Gita daily with supreme faith and devotion realises the world of Rudra or Lord Shiva," Lord Vishnu revealed. "He becomes a Gana in Lord Shiva's army of attendants and lives in Mount Kailash).*

*Adhyaayam shlokapaadam vaa nityam yah pathate narah; Sa yaati narataam yaavanmanwantaram vasundhare.*

*(O Earth, even if a person reads a part of the Gita daily by even reciting a verse daily, he retains a human body till the end of a Manvantara that amounts to 71 Mahayugas or 308,448,000 years).*

*Geetaayaah shloka dashakam sapta pancha chatushtayam; Dwautreenekam tadardhamvaa shlokaanaam yah pathennarah.*

*Chandralokam avaapnoti varshaanaam ayutam dhruvam;*
*Geetaapaathasamaayukto mrito maanushataam vrajet.*

*(The one who repeats ten, seven, five, four, three, two verses or even one or half a verse daily attains the region of the moon and lives there for 10,000 years. When a man is used to studying the Bhagavad Gita daily, a dying man comes back to life again as a human being).*

*Geetaabhyaasam punah kritwaa labhate muktim uttamaam;*
*Geetetyucchaarasamyukto mriyamaano gatim labhet.*

*(A man attains liberation by the repeated study of the Gita. When he utters the word Gita at the time of death, a person attains liberation).*

***Geetaarthashravanaasakto mahaapaapayuto'pi vaa; Vaikuntham samavaapnoti vishnunaa saha modate.***

***(Even if one is full of sins, the person who is ever eager to learn the true meaning of the Gita, travels to the kingdom of God and re-joins with me).***

***Geetaartham dhyaayate nityam kritwaa karmaani bhoorishah; Jeevanmuktah sa vijneyo dehaante paramam padam.***

***(The one who meditates on the meaning of the Gita, after the performance of several actions, attains the supreme goal after his death. Such an individual is considered as a true Jivanmukta).***

A Jivanmukta is the person who has attained liberation while still living.

***Geetaam aashritya bahavo bhoobhujo janakaadayah; Nirdhootakalmashaa loke geetaa yaataah param padam.***

***(After seeking refuge in the Gita, many kings of this world like Janaka have reached the highest state or goal that Man can reach, and have been purified of all sins).***

***Geetaayaah pathanam kritwaa maahaatmyam naiva yah pathet; Vrithaa paatho bhavet tasya shrama eva hyudaahritah.***

***(The person who fails to read this 'Glory of the Gita' even after reading the Bhagavad Gita, loses the benefit gained by the act, and all that remains is the effort).***

*By this statement, Lord Vishnu wishes to test and confirm the faith of the reader in the Bhagavad Gita, which is not a mere philosophical book but the word of God Himself. Hence, it should be studied with great faith and devotion. 'The Gita Mahatmya'or 'The Glory of the Gita' generates this very devotion in one's heart.*

*Etanmaahaatmyasamyuktam geetaabhyaasam karoti yah; Sa tatphalamavaapnoti durlabhaam gatim aapnuyaat.*

*(The one who studies the Gita, together with this "Glory of the Gita", attains the fruits that are mentioned above, and also reaches the Supreme state which is otherwise impossible for a man to attain).*

*Suta Uvaacha: Maahaatmyam etad geetaayaah mayaa proktam sanaatanam; Geetaante cha pathedyastu yaduktam tatphalam labhet.*

*(Suta said: "This greatness of the Glory of the Gita is everlasting, and should be read after the study of the Gita, as narrated by Me to obtain the fruits mentioned in it).*

*Iti srivaraahapuraane srigeetaamaahaatmyam sampoornam.*

*(Thus ends the "Glory of the Gita", narrated by Lord Vishnu and found in the Varaha Purana).*

*Om Shanti, Shanti, Shanti!*

# More Books on Indian Mythology